SURVIVING AN EATING DISORDER

SURVIVING AN EATING DISORDER

Strategies for Family and Friends

MICHELE SIEGEL, PH.D.
JUDITH BRISMAN, PH.D.
MARGOT WEINSHEL, M.S.W.

HarperPerennial
A Division of HarperCollins*Publishers*

A hardcover edition of this book was published in 1988 by Harper & Row, Publishers.

 For information address Harper & Row, Publishers, Inc., 10 East 53rd Street, New York, N.Y. 10022. Published simultaneously in Canada by Fitzhenry & Whiteside Limited, Toronto.

FIRST PERENNIAL LIBRARY EDITION PUBLISHED 1989.

Library of Congress Cataloging-in-Publication Data

Siegel, Michele.
Surviving an eating disorder.

"Perennial Library."
Bibliography: p.
Includes index.
1. Appetite disorders—Patients—Family relationships.
I. Brisman, Judith. II. Weinshel, Margot. III. Title.
RC552.E18S54 1989 616.85′2 87-45668
ISBN 0-06-091553-6 (pbk.)

---

96 97 RRD 20 19 18 17

To our patients and their families who, in their willingness to share their struggles, have asked us the questions and taught us the answers

CONTENTS

ACKNOWLEDGMENTS

As therapists, we were often approached by people who worried that someone they knew was eating disordered. Parents, relatives, and friends would ask us, "Isn't there something I can read that will help me know what to do? I feel so helpless." While we could recommend books about eating disorders, there was no book we could suggest that would tell them what they could do to help.

This book was written to answer these questions. By bringing our accumulated knowledge and diverse experiences with eating disorders and with families to the writing of this book, we offer you specific guidelines on how to survive an eating disorder.

Drs. Michele Siegel and Judith Brisman are psychoanalytically trained psychologists. They are the founders of Bulimia Treatment Associates (BTA), a private outpatient facility for the treatment of eating disorders located in New York City. Michele Siegel is the Director of Clinical Services and Judith Brisman is the Director of Training. Margot Weinshel is a social worker trained in family therapy. She is a faculty member of the Ackerman Institute for Family Therapy in New York City and has been a consultant to BTA. We are all in private practice in Manhattan.

Over a period of three years, we talked, wrote, argued, and

learned from one another. The blending of our backgrounds and the give-and-take of our discussions allowed the project to grow beyond our original conception. The result is bigger than any of our single contributions.

We all owe a debt of gratitude to the educators, supervisors, and institutes who facilitated our professional growth and helped pave the way to the writing of this book. We wish to acknowledge Hilde Bruch, M.D., for her enduring contribution to the understanding of eating disorders and to Salvador Minuchin, M.D., for his pioneering work in treating families with anorexia.

There are many people whose help contributed greatly to this book. First of all, we wish to thank our agent, Frances Goldin, for believing in us when our idea was just taking shape. Our heartfelt appreciation goes to our editor at Harper & Row, Janet Goldstein. With a firm hand but light touch, she cleared the way so that we could bring to fruition everything we had to give to the project. She brought us far beyond our own expectations.

Our colleagues gave generously of their time and expertise in reading our first draft and giving their suggestions. Charles Murkofsky, M.D., Nancy Bravman, M.S.W, Judy Rabinor, Ph.D., Jackie McSweeney, B.A., Vivian Hanson Meehan, R.N., B.A., and Howard Weiss, Ph.D., were dedicated and sensitive in illuminating the strengths and weaknesses of the manuscript. Their advice added immeasurably to the strengths of the book. A special thanks to Michael Kimmel, Ph.D., for his attention to the project, his openness and perceptive comments, all of which helped the book take shape. Much thanks also to John Drimmer for his consistent support and invaluable reminders of how the creative process works.

We would also like to thank our colleagues in related disciplines for reviewing the sections of the book relevant to their expertise. Our thanks to Robert Bernstein, M.D., for reviewing the medical sections, Lyle Rosnick, M.D., for adding to the psychiatric portions of the text, Peter Sirosi, M.D., for his review of the text relevant to gynecology, and Peter Aborn, D.D.S., for contributing to the section on dentistry.

A special thanks to Irv Barocas whose helpful work on the manuscript endured from the beginning to the end of the project.

We would also like to thank Michelle Morgan and Martha McCrary whose typing and organizational skills allowed us to survive the early stages of the manuscript.

Jane R. Hirschmann, M.S.W., was particularly helpful early on in sharing with us her own experiences and knowledge about getting a book off the ground.

A very special thanks to Marcia Richards whose skills as a typist and whose willingness to give up a night's sleep on a moment's notice saved us many deadlines.

We would like to thank Irv Barocas and Robert, Rebecca, and Josh Bazell for their continual support throughout the writing of the book.

We are particularly grateful to Jesse Barocas who put off his birth until two weeks before the end of the deadline.

Finally, we want to thank each other. Collaborating on a book has been an incredible experience for us all. We acknowledge each other's skills, dedication, perseverance, and, most importantly, sense of humor which carried us through the ups and downs over the long haul of this project.

The first-person stories and case examples in this book accurately reflect the feelings, experiences, and circumstances expressed by patients, their families, and friends, but all names, locales, and identifying details have been changed.

SURVIVING AN EATING DISORDER

INTRODUCTION

How to Survive

This book is written for all of you who are living with or in a relationship with someone who has an eating problem. Perhaps you are a parent, spouse, or sibling of the person with the problem. You may be a lover, roommate, colleague, or friend. You may already know that a disorder exists because signs of the problem are obvious, or a doctor or therapist may have diagnosed it. Or, you may be aware of peculiar eating and/or weight problems but not know if a serious disorder is present. The person you know may or may not already be involved in some kind of treatment. As readers, you come to this book from a wide range of experiences with the sufferer.

Yours is a difficult position to be in. You want to help, but you're not sure what is best. You may be witness to many behaviors that are destructive and frightening, as well as disruptive to a household or a relationship. Not knowing what to do can make you feel helpless and confused.

When faced with such difficult times, the temptation is often to make the other person stop—stop bingeing, stop starving, stop vomiting, stop exercising. You may be setting up rewards for weight lost—or weight gained; perhaps you are keeping charts and records; you try to talk nicely, you plead, you get angry and "set down the law." In most cases this makes the problem much worse. You end up in a control battle that you will inevitably lose.

Sometimes these tactics may work. You may be able to control someone else's behavior or coerce a change—but it won't help for long. The person may stop the behaviors for fear of reprisals, or may just become better at keeping them secret. In either case, change will not be sustained. External forces may work temporarily—but once the force is removed, the motivation to change is lost.

When you try to control the eating behaviors, you not only prolong the problem, but there are other costs as well. This focus leaves you entangled in battles over food that result in the neglect of other parts of your relationship. Activities in your own life are frequently subsumed.

Because you are not the one with the actual problem, however, your own difficulties may be overlooked. *Your* suffering and confusion about how to proceed may very well go unnoticed or untreated. People in your position can easily become the silent sufferers—the unseen victims of the eating disorder.

This book is written for you. We will talk about what you can do to help, what you can expect from the eating disordered person—and yourself, how you can improve your relationship with the person you care about, and what sort of support is available during these difficult times.

This book is about recovery—not only that of the eating disordered person, but your recovery and the recovery of your relationship as well.

In general, it is best to read the book in the order presented. The beginning chapters on "Gaining Perspective" provide the basis for understanding the philosophy behind the interventions we suggest in later chapters, "Confronting the Problem" and "Using New Strategies."

However, some of you may have immediate questions that you need answered before reading the entire book. For example, if the person you care about is already in treatment, but mealtimes are a horror, go directly to Chapter 7. If you think you are facing a life-threatening situation and don't know whom to speak to about this, see Chapter 6 on "Seeking Help." If you have just been told to "Mind your own business" and you don't know what to do now, see Chapters 4 and 5. You can return to the rest of the book after your more pressing questions have been addressed.

Part I, "Gaining Perspective," provides information that will broaden your understanding of the sufferer and his or her experiences. While both sexes suffer from eating disorders, women are affected in greater numbers. In order to avoid the awkward use of *he* and *she* throughout this book, we will be using *she* when speaking generally about the sufferer. What you are seeing and what the behaviors may mean are explored in Chapters 1 through 3. In particular, Chapter 1, "What You See," acquaints you with the overt signs of the three major eating disorders: anorexia, bulimia, and compulsive overeating. Signs of trouble and the progression of the disorders are described.

Chapter 2, "Hidden Feelings," examines the inner experiences of the sufferer, aspects of the eating disorder that you cannot see. Chapter 3, "The Family Picture," describes the family context in which the problem develops and is sustained. These chapters develop the idea that an eating disorder is not merely a problem with food and weight, but one that involves complex psychological factors. This perspective provides the groundwork for the changes we suggest you make in later chapters.

Part II of the book is "Confronting the Problem." If you suspect (or know) that someone has a problem with food, do you say anything? If so, what do you say—and how do you say it? Chapter 4 answers these questions and guides you in breaking the silence about the problem and approaching the person whom you believe is in trouble. But what if you are met with anger and denial? There are certain things you can (and should) do—there are also limits to how you can be of help. Chapter 5 addresses these issues. Recovery most often involves outside support. Chapter 6 focuses on the process of seeking outside support and treatment, both for you and the eating-disordered person.

The last part of the book, Part III, "Using New Strategies," discusses the specifics of what you can do to make your situation better. Inevitably when you are involved with someone with an eating problem, there are practical questions regarding how to handle food and weight issues. Do you keep sweets in the house? What do you say if she asks you if she looks fat? Should you make her eat dinner? These are the types of questions that are answered in Chapter 7. This chapter will help you untangle yourself from the struggles with food and weight, while the person with the eating disorder remains responsible for her actions and the consequences of her behavior. This is not easy to do. Disentangling yourself from an eating disorder is a complicated process. In Chapter 8, we ease the process of disengagement by offering new perspectives on your involvement in the problem. Finally, in Chapter 9, we consider the aspects of your relationship with the eating-disordered person that may have been overlooked. How do you talk to each other? How are responsibilities shared? Are freedoms and privacy in the relationship respected? When was the last time you had fun? By exploring and changing areas in your relationship outside the arena of food, you open the door to new growth, respect, and enjoyment in your relationship.

Surviving an Eating Disorder can be used as a general reference book to pick up whenever you are faced with the question "What do I do now?" However, this is not just a guidebook. *Surviving an Eating Disorder* examines eating problems with the goal of broadening your perspective on the difficulties you see and furthering your understanding of the complex syndromes of anorexia, bulimia, and compulsive overeating. The combination of perspectives and strategies offered in this book can provide you with a new and richer awareness of both the eating disorder and your relationship with the person you care about.

PART I

Gaining Perspective

1

WHAT YOU SEE:
The Behavioral Aspects of Eating Disorders

I looked over at my 14-year-old daughter, Lara, as the internist spoke to us about the causes of Lara's recent fainting spells. "Anorexic. Your daughter is anorexic." I watched Lara cross her sticklike arms in reaction to these words. Her face suddenly looked old to me, bony, unpleasantly pointed. My heart sank. I have failed her, I thought. What did I do wrong? Lara was a straight A student. She never seemed like she had any problems on her mind. How could she be anorexic? No, this is a mistake. Someone has made a mistake.

Barbara L., 39-year-old mother

I came home early from work with flowers, thinking I'd surprise my wife. When I put the key in the door, I was met with a frantic cry, "Wait, who is it? Ben? Don't come in yet! Wait!" I panicked—I thought the worst and raced into the apartment. And there was Nina, standing in the middle of the kitchen. Several boxes of cakes, cookies, and a pie were opened and half eaten. Candy wrappers were strewn over the floor. The refrigerator door hung wide open. A puddle of spilt milk rested in the middle of the table; ice cream was melting in the container beside it. Nina looked at me angrily. "Why didn't you call?" she demanded. "Why are you home so early?" A moment before I had been so sure I would find her with another man—but this? This didn't make *any* sense to me—in a frightening way, it felt worse. What had I walked in on? What was happening to my wife? I remember not knowing what to do with the flowers.

Ben, 27-year-old husband

It's getting harder and harder living with Jennie. It's almost like living with two different people. Half the time she is on some diet or other, following it to the T, not an inch of leeway. Then suddenly she's eating like a madwoman, and it's possible that at any time all the food in the house can disappear. During these times she won't go out, she'll break plans with me continuously and will look miserable and depressed. All she wants to talk about is what she's eaten, how "good" she's been, or how different life will be at a low weight. She could stand to lose weight—she's about 180 pounds. But even when she does get thinner, which happens periodically, it seems that starts the whole cycle over again. Jennie's my best friend but I've had enough. Is there something I can do?

Pamela, 24-year-old roommate

WHEN EATING HABITS BECOME EATING DISORDERS

The mother, husband, and friend in the above examples knew that something was wrong. What they were seeing was not normal behavior. The people they were involved with were in trouble. In all three cases, there were clear signs that someone was eating disordered.

When an eating disorder exists, it is recognized by certain behaviors, the most noticeable being an obsession with food and weight. This obsession can take the form of binge eating, starving, vomiting, compulsive exercising, or other behaviors focused on eating, getting rid of, or avoiding food.

Eating disorders however are not merely problems with food. They are psychological disorders, many aspects of which are not apparent to an outside observer.

It is often not easy to tell who is and who is not suffering with an eating disorder. Dieting, exercising, fasting, and a preoccupation with food and weight are so much a part of our culture that it is unusual to find a teenage girl or woman who is not or has not been concerned with weight. It only takes a glance at the covers of women's magazines to see the relentless focus on staying slim. However, these magazines do not offer the single value of slimness—they communicate a double message. These same magazines also feature recipes for rich, enticing desserts. Our culture seems to encourage us all to "have our cake and eat it too." Men, too, are becoming increasingly food and weight conscious, as we see when we look at the growing numbers of marathon runners, body builders, and fitness enthusiasts. We have only to look at the cosmetics newly available to men, such as Clinique products, to see that men are no longer excluded from the society's emphasis on good looks.

The focus on body, dieting, and weight is particularly acute among teenagers. Teenage girls are constantly vying to be the thinnest, or skipping meals to lose weight. Talking about eating, overeating, or even group "pigouts" are communal experiences. Regardless of the age group, it seems food and weight are on everyone's mind. Does this then mean that everyone in our society has an eating disorder? No.

An eating disorder exists when one's attitude toward food and weight has gone awry—when one's feelings about work, school, relationships, day-to-day activities, and one's experience of emotional well-being are determined by what has or has not been eaten or by a number on the scale. Most of us know what it is like to comfort or reward ourselves with food, to allow ourselves an indulgent meal after a particularly difficult day, to have the extra calories when we feel disappointed. Most of us know how it feels to wish we looked a little thinner in that bathing suit or to want to look particularly good for an important occasion. However, when these wishes or rewards turn into the basis of all decisions, when the pounds prevent us from going to the beach, when our looks are more important than the occasion itself, then there are indications of a problem deserving attention.

Eating problems usually start out with the common wish to lose weight and maintain a certain body image. These are concerns that most of us have experienced. Often people can go through a period of intensive dieting, obsession with weight, or overeating that will be short-lived and end without outside interventions. However, a potentially short-lived bout with food control becomes an eating disorder when the eating behaviors are no longer used merely to maintain or reduce weight. An eating habit becomes an eating disorder when the primary need it satisfies is psychological, not physical. The eating behavior then becomes a vehicle for the expression of problems *outside* the arena of calories.

Someone who is eating disordered does not eat because she is physically hungry. She eats for reasons unrelated to physiological needs. That is, the eating may temporarily block out painful feelings, calm anxiety, subdue tensions. Or she may starve, not because she is full, but because she wants to control her bodily needs.

Consider Corey's situation for a moment. Corey is a 28-year-old who came to us for help. When Corey was a teenager and became upset because of a school event or a canceled date, she found it comforting to sit in front of the television and slowly savor a piece of chocolate cake or other dessert from her mother's well-stocked kitchen. During this time, she was of normal weight. While she always enjoyed her late night snacks, they were certainly not the focus of her thinking or plans.

When Corey left home to go to college, however, she began to have more trying times. She felt somewhat overwhelmed by the demands of living on her own in a new environment. Frequently, she felt homesick. More and more often, she looked forward to the late night snacks (which actually began to occur earlier and earlier in the evening). She found the food soothing and she could block out her thoughts when she ate. As the school year progressed, Corey found herself thinking about and looking forward to eating as soon as she woke up. Her thoughts started to revolve around what she would eat at mealtimes and what snacks she could buy throughout the day.

She was soon feeling that the rest of her life was secondary to eating. The consequent weight gain accelerated Corey's withdrawal from her social life to a world of food. At this point, Corey could no longer be considered a normally "food-obsessed" teenager; her focus on food, her social withdrawal, and the compulsive eating behaviors were all signs that her eating habits were now part of an eating disorder.

Karla, on the other hand, could be considered to be eating disordered from the early age of 13. As soon as she began to develop physically, Karla recalls, the natural roundness of her shape led her to worry about becoming overweight and she started to control her food intake and weight. She decided that at 5′ 2″ it was okay to weigh 95 pounds, absolutely no more (and she found it too difficult to weigh less). Since age 13, Karla has remained 95 pounds. She is now 30 years old. She weighs herself six to ten times daily. If her weight fluctuates at all and rises above 95 pounds, she will do anything possible to make the scale show 95 again. Her efforts include exercising rigorously throughout the day and night (sometimes until 3:00 or 4:00 A.M., when her weight finally returns to 95 pounds), sitting in a sauna wrapped in Saran Wrap (to sweat out the liquids), and certainly not eating or drinking anything (including water) until the scale again reaches the magical number 95. If Karla has anything planned for a day when her weight happens to be 96 pounds, she will either cancel the event or know that she will have a bad time. When asked, "How can you know you will have a bad time at a party before you get there?" Karla answers simply, "Because I'm 96 pounds and feel fat." Karla's rigid attitude certainly signals the clinical picture of an eating disorder—that is, one's experience of day-to-day situations are rigidly determined by one's weight and food intake.

THE EATING DISORDERS

When people talk about "eating disorders," they are usually referring to either anorexia nervosa, bulimia, or compulsive overeating—or some combination of the three. The sections which follow will describe the signs and signals characteristic of each disorder.

Checklists are included at the end of this chapter to help you recognize and identify signs of trouble. Your understanding of the disorders will help you confront the problem and get the professional help that is needed. (Further information is provided in Chapters 4 and 6.) The better informed you are about what you see, the better able you will be to discuss your concerns openly, clearly, and in a manner that can be helpful.

Anorexia

Anorexia is characterized by a significant weight loss due to a purposeful attempt to stop eating. The anorexic, intensely fearful of becoming obese, considers herself to be fat—no matter what her actual weight. Anorexics close to death at 65 pounds will show you where on their bodies they feel they need to lose weight. In an attempt to be even skinnier, the anorexic avoids taking in calories at all costs—even if the cost is her life.

ESSENTIAL FEATURES OF ANOREXIA NERVOSA

- Intense fear of becoming obese, which does not diminish as weight loss progresses.
- Disturbance of body image, e.g., claiming to "feel fat" even when emaciated.
- Significant weight loss (at least 25 percent of normal body weight).
- Refusal to maintain a minimal normal body weight.
- No known physical illness that would account for the weight loss.
- Amenorrhea (loss of menstruation).

Mariel's diary revealed the drastic nature of her dieting. When she was 16 years old and anorexic, she would write a daily entry in her diary listing the food she ate each day.

This entry is typical:

10 A.M.	1 cup black coffee
	Sweet & Low
Noon	1 cup black coffee
	Sweet & Low
2 P.M.	1 vitamin A
	1 multiple vitamin
	1 vitamin B
7 P.M.	1 bouillon cube chicken broth and hot water
	1 Dietetic jello —1 cup

Mariel was 72 pounds and 5′ 6″. That she had already passed out twice by the time of this entry was no impediment to her harsh regime.

The attempt to lose weight usually occurs through induced starvation, but anorexics can accelerate weight loss or undo the damage of occasional binges by vomiting, taking laxatives, using diuretics, or exercising rigorously. Someone is diagnosed as anorexic if she is at least 25 percent below her normal body weight. Thus if someone at 5′ is considered to be at a normal weight at 100 pounds, she would be considered anorexic if her weight dropped to 75 pounds.

Amenorrhea always occurs in anorexia (often before a significant amount of weight has been lost). Loss of menstruation combined with attempts at dieting and an intense fear of becoming fat is a sign that anorexia is the problem, even before body weight has dropped significantly below normal.

Katie was a 5′ 4″ 16-year-old who gained 25 pounds over six months following the breakup of a relationship with her boyfriend. In reaction to the loss of the relationship, she overate daily, avoiding friends and her usual social life. When she reached 145 pounds, however, she panicked at the weight gain and stopped eating. At home she would pick at her food, calculating the calories of each bite. What she actually put into her mouth was negligible. She insisted on eating only salads, and after meals would figure out how many hours of exercise she needed to do that night to work off the fat. Sometimes she'd be up for hours before she felt she had burned off the calories. Within six weeks, Katie lost the weight she had gained as well as an additional 15 pounds. She was now 5′ 4″ and 105 pounds and she wanted to lose more weight.

While Katie had not yet lost 25 percent of her normal body weight, her behavior was signaling a problem. The refusal to eat, seeing herself as overweight despite her low weight, and her preoccupation with food and exercise were serious warning flags of anorexia.

Katie did in fact continue on a downhill course for about six months until a combination of individual and family psychotherapy reversed the direction of her persistent weight loss. After she had been in therapy for a few months, Katie admitted that at 105 pounds she had already begun missing her periods, but had kept that information secret, fearing her parents would make her eat. Even though Katie's weight had not dropped to 80 or 90 pounds, she was no doubt anorexic.

HOW IT BEGINS

No one starts a diet with the intention of becoming anorexic. The young woman who may ultimately find herself emaciated and near death starts out dieting like anyone else who wants to lose weight. However, for the person who is to become anorexic, the dieting and weight loss quickly take on a function that is unanticipated and unplanned. As this person begins to lose weight, she feels a newfound control in a life in which she previously did not feel effective or strong. Suddenly she feels powerful—she is able to make herself lose weight and look good. She does not have to give in to her hunger. She is someone who doesn't have to eat like other people do.

"When I'd be at dinner with my friends," says Margie, 17, of her months of anorexia, "I'd feel superior to everyone who was eating. I felt like I was the only one in control. The others were slaves to their hunger. It made me feel better than them."

The dieting and weight loss give meaning to the anorexic's life. Each day is a challenge—and every morning the number on the scale will say whether she has won or lost the previous day's contest. This challenge, this power, is not something that is a planned intention of the dieter but, once in effect, is hard for the anorexic to give up. The anorexic has often been the "good girl," accommodating to what others want of her. Now, perhaps for the first time, she has found a behavior that says, "You can't make me do what you want me to do. I'm not giving in to you—or to my hunger—or to my feelings. I'll eat what *I* want."

For the normally unassuming and shy anorexic, this is not an easy stance to abandon.

WHO IS VULNERABLE

The overwhelming majority—95 percent—of anorexics are women. The age of onset is usually between 12 to 18 years, but anorexia does occur in women in their 40s and 50s. As many as 1 in 250 young women have anorexia.[1]

Someone who becomes anorexic is vulnerable to this disorder because she has not developed sufficient means of feeling competent, worthy, and effective. The preanorectic is often the model child, rarely complaining, usually very helpful, compliant, and eager to please. Her school performance is usually above average and she is highly demanding and critical of herself. In essence, she is someone who has learned to put others' needs ahead of her own and who feels that in order to be cared about she must win the approval of others—even if this means squelching her feelings or acting in ways that don't feel comfortable.

The anorexic strives to be perfect and her emphasis on perfection, in combination with the impossibility of achieving it, leads her to strenuous and relentless attempts to do better. This is not a child with a comfortable sense of her own abilities, but rather one who always has to prove her competence. She is often very private and

1. *Diagnostic Statistical Manual of Mental Disorders*, 3rd Edition (Washington, D.C.: American Psychiatric Association, 1980).

keeps her feelings to herself, misleading others that all is well. But beneath the false facade, there is deep trouble.

"I never felt like we really asked much of Zoe," Mrs. Camden told us. "We didn't have to. She was always so bright and fun to be with—and very responsible. If Zoe had chores or responsibilities around the house, you knew they'd be done. You could count on it. She never complained like her brother or sisters. I never would have thought anything was wrong. Zoe's anorexia was a shock to everyone." At the time Mrs. Camden spoke with us, Zoe, 15, was in an intensive care unit because of kidney failure secondary to the anorexia.

HOW THE DISORDER PROGRESSES

Once dieting has begun to serve a psychological function, there are characteristic behaviors that you might notice. There will be a preoccupation with food, dieting, and weight loss. However, weight loss is not the only criterion. People who are *not* anorexic sometimes lose a lot of weight due to depression or a physical disorder, such as an intestinal problem. These problems may go undiagnosed and will result in the same type of extreme weight loss one sees in the anorexic. The difference is that in these cases the person is not actively attempting to be thinner. Whenever extreme weight loss occurs, a doctor should be contacted to rule out physical disorders or a psychological depression that might be the cause. Only in the case of an eating disorder will you see an active attempt at weight loss.

Someone who is anorexic will ask you if she looks fat. She will feel ashamed of being seen in public—because, at 80 pounds, she feels "disgustingly overweight." She may be on the scale ten times a day.

Her diets will grow more and more extreme as time goes on. Often the anorexic will start with a normal diet and then eliminate one or two foods each day. If she can keep doing this, she feels pleased, sometimes elated that she has met her goals—if not, she is devastated, forlorn, hateful of herself "for being such a pig."

When Suzanne, 21, first came to treatment she spoke of her experience this way:

> Yesterday, for example, I had a grapefruit and black coffee for breakfast, and for dinner I had the normal salad I eat every night. I always skip lunch. I had promised myself that I would only eat three-quarters of the salad since I've been feeling stuffed after it lately—but I think I ate more than the three-quarters. I know it was just lettuce and broccoli but I can't believe I did that. I was up all night worrying about getting fat.

Anorexics' conversations often center around food or looks. In fact, despite her own starvation, the anorexic often enjoys cooking, preparing meals for others, and collecting recipes. While she won't eat, her unattended feelings of hunger and deprivation will result in constant thoughts about food. Many anorexics will even hide and hoard the food they won't eat.

Mrs. Jansen was looking through her daughter Jennie's bureau drawers for clothes to bring her after she had left for a three-month hospitalization for anorexia. She was surprised to find one drawer packed with high-calorie sweets. It was a shock to Mrs. Jansen that Jennie could starve herself to near death and keep all that food at her fingertips.

Another particularly disturbing hallmark of anorexia is the persistent denial that anything is wrong. Hunger and fatigue are strongly denied. So are the physiological complications secondary to the disorder. Common medical problems which the anorexic ignores are dizziness, numbness to hands and feet, dehydration, and low blood pressure. Heart irregularities or heart or kidney failure can occur as a result of potassium depletion and severe nutritional imbalances. Loss of concentration is also common. Despite this, anorexics are typically fiercely resistant to the idea of therapy because all attempts to help or intervene are seen as a way to make them eat.

As a result of the ferocity of the anorexic's denial and her tenacious hold on the disorder, the progression of anorexia can be tragic. Some women die. Various studies estimate the fatality rate to be between 2 and 21 percent.[2]

For some people anorexia can become a chronic problem, almost a way of life, with the sufferer never regaining a healthy weight and living a life tormented by the terror of becoming obese and driven by compulsions to exercise and eat ritualistically. For most people who become anorexic, however, the disorder is an acute illness lasting months to a few years that can be treated effectively through a combination of psychological and medical care.

Bulimia

Bulimia is usually characterized by bingeing, that is eating large amounts of food in a short time. The binge is followed by an attempt to get rid of the food and consequent calories, in what is called the "purge." In some cases, the person doesn't binge per se but feels compelled to get rid of anything she's eaten beyond what she's decided is okay to live with.

"When I dieted, bread was absolutely out of the question," says Lucy, now 24 years old, of her adolescent bulimic years.

> If I had *one* bite of bread, just one, I felt as though I blew it! I'd stop listening to whomever was talking to me at the table. I'd start thinking, *How can I get rid of this?* I'd worry about how fat I'd look, how I couldn't fit into my clothes. My head would be flooded with thoughts of what to do now—should I binge since I'd already blown it? I had to undo what I'd done. The night was blown. I was a mess.

You cannot tell that someone is bulimic by her weight. Bulimics may be slightly underweight or overweight, but are usually within

2. K. M. Bemis, "Current approaches to the etiology and treatment of anorexia nervosa," *Psychological Bulletin* 85, 3 (1978): 593–617. See also L. K. G. Hsu, A. H. Crisp, and B. Harding, "Outcome of anorexia nervosa," *The Lancet* (1979): 61–65.

a normal range. However, within this range, you might see 10- to 15-pound weight fluctuations.

When someone is not bingeing or purging, the way she eats may vary. Some bulimics eat normally, others diet rigorously at all times. Regardless of what is being eaten, most bulimic women never feel comfortable around food. Food is the enemy and they are engaged in a constant battle.

ESSENTIAL FEATURES OF BULIMIA

- Episodic binge eating accompanied by an awareness that the eating pattern is abnormal.
- Repeated attempts to lose weight by severely restrictive diets, self-induced vomiting, use of laxatives, cathartics, enemas, colonics or diuretics, or excessive exercise.
- Fear of not being able to stop eating voluntarily.
- Depressed mood.
- Self-deprecating thoughts following eating binges.

THE BINGE. A binge usually refers to the rapid consumption of a large amount of high-caloric food in a relatively short time. Binges can range anywhere from 1000 to 60,000 calories. However, sometimes a bulimic will consider a small amount of food (such as a piece of cake) to be a "binge." A binge can consist of just about anything you can imagine and may depend on what's available in terms of food and/or finances. Some people will binge occasionally, while for others bingeing will take up a major portion of every day.

Some bulimics go to restaurants, order a full-course meal, throw up, then go to another restaurant and eat again. Three or four full-size meals can be eaten before the person feels exhausted enough to return home. And yes, it can be terribly costly. We have treated some women whose addiction to food was so extreme that the binges cost them upwards of $60 to $70 a day. When the binges are this costly or when money is not readily available (such as in the case of a child or a teenager), the bulimic may steal to support her food habit. In the most extreme cases, women have prostituted themselves to keep the food habit going.

Bingeing usually occurs in secret. It may be planned in advance, or it may be the case that any unplanned eating, even one bite, can lead to the feeling that the damage has been done. The bulimic is always trying to control her urges to eat. The consequent feelings of deprivation or the upset she feels when any control is relinquished often precipitates a binge.

Once a binge begins, bulimics will ravage their kitchen for food, go to the grocery store, or order in food from local restaurants. Or they will find food in other ways. One shy 18-year-old told us that when she vacationed with her parents, she'd steal food from the room service carts in the hallways of hotels. Another woman, a Wall Street executive who dressed impeccably and was very polite and well-mannered, described nightmarish evenings of rummaging for food through garbage bins in the back halls of her apartment building. She resorted to this behavior because she had ordered in food so often in the middle of the night that she could no longer stand her feelings of humiliation when met with her doorman's puzzled looks.

When a binge takes place, all feelings are blocked out. The food acts as an anesthetic. As one bulimic woman put it:

> I go to never-never land. Once I start bingeing, it's like being in a stupor, like being drunk. Nothing else matters. Heaven help the person who tries to stop me. It's like I'm a different person. It's very humiliating—but not then, not while I'm eating. While I'm eating, *nothing* else matters.

AFTER THE BINGE: SHAME AND PANIC. The binge leaves the bulimic exhausted and uncomfortable—not just physically uncomfortable, but emotionally uncomfortable as well. She is besieged with feelings of shame and guilt. She doesn't recognize the person she becomes during the binge and despises herself. She loathes this out-of-control, needy person. As one client expressed it, "I can't believe I can turn into a creature that acts in such an animal-like way."

Bulimics consider their bingeing disgusting and are deeply ashamed of it. It goes against the grain of who they are and what they are striving to be.

In addition to being ashamed, they are also terrified about weight gain from whatever has been eaten, regardless of whether or not a large amount of food has been consumed. Bulimics are so perfectionistic in their standards of themselves that weight gain from the binge is never tolerated. They fear that any extra pounds will expose their other side, the person who binges and loses control. This is a frightening thought.

As Mary Anna, 28, told us:

> I would die if people knew. If they even thought for one moment that I wasn't this perfect, well-tuned professional machine. If I gained weight, they'd see something was wrong—it would be a tip-off. I can't let anyone see how needy and desperate I get.

The awful feelings of shame, panic about weight gain, and the physical discomfort lead the bulimic to the purge—the means of undoing the damage of the binge.

THE PURGE. Purging can take different forms. Most often it involves vomiting or laxative abuse. Other forms of purging include the use of diuretics, enemas, colonics, fasting, strict dieting, rigorous exercising, diet pills, and/or amphetamine or cocaine abuse (these latter to suppress hunger on days following a binge).

The amount of purging varies from person to person. Some people binge and vomit a few times a month, others over twenty times a day. Sometimes the vomiting is induced in the middle of a binge so the eating can continue. Other times the person vomits only after all the food has been consumed. Vomiting as a solution begins benignly, almost by accident, and only gradually becomes a ritualistic part of the bulimic cycle.

For Julia, vomiting was a "solution" to her struggle to keep her weight down. She had been thin as a child, but during adolescence her body filled out and she became self-conscious about her size. By the time she left for college, she was about 15 pounds overweight, and those 15 pounds felt like a major barrier to her self-confidence. Away from home and the seduction of her mother's kitchen, Julia made a commitment to diet and she stuck to it. Julia rigidly stayed on her food plan for three months and steadily approached her desired goal of 110 pounds.

By spring of her first college year, she thought of herself as a "new person." She had a new body, a new wardrobe—and a new-found terror of regaining weight. She couldn't stay on the diet forever. "I remember coming home from a party. I had eaten a lot there and I felt fat and disgusting. I don't know why I thought of it then, but I remembered some friend of mine telling me how she threw up to lose weight. I decided to try it. I didn't really let myself think too much about what I was going to do or else it would have seemed too disgusting. But I used my fingers and then it was done. I felt so relieved, so thin. I couldn't believe it was that easy. It was like magic."

For bulimics the purge is the antidote to their loss of control over food. As one patient put it, "When I binge, I lose. When I purge, the food loses."

In all cases, the vomiting is induced—it doesn't "just happen." At first, vomiting is forced—by using fingers, a spoon handle, or Ipecac (an over-the-counter drug usually used by parents to induce vomiting in their children after accidental poisoning). After repeated vomiting, however, the esophageal muscles relax so much that many women don't have to do anything but tighten their stomachs and they will be able to bring up the food.

The use of laxatives as a purging technique usually begins when someone takes one to two laxatives to get rid of the feeling that her stomach is full. Most laxative abusers have difficulty vomiting and turn to this method instead. The irony about laxative abuse is that by the time the laxatives work, the food has already been digested and the calories absorbed. Thus, laxative use gives the illusion of weight loss (since water weight is lost) but in actuality, calories are still retained and weight is put on.

Yet even when laxative users know this, they often continue the abuse as a means of "feeling" thinner or flattening their stomach by purging themselves of water in the body. They refuse to believe it isn't working to control weight. Laxative use quickly becomes laxative abuse. The body builds a tolerance and one or two tablets a day quickly lose their effectiveness. Often by the time a bulimic seeks help, she may be taking anywhere from 20 to 200 laxatives daily.

Enemas, diuretics, and colonics are used like laxatives to eliminate a feeling of fullness but are ineffective in reducing calorie intake. They begin the use of these purging techniques to facilitate or speed up the body's usual functioning.

Other forms of purging (diet pills, drug use, fasting and/or rigorous exercise) are used to inhibit eating or to burn off the calories after a binge.

John, 24, one of the male bulimics seen through our center, had a pattern of bingeing continuously for a week or two following a disappointment or frustration in his life. During this time, he ate throughout the day, would miss work, stopped shaving and caring for himself, and could easily put on 20 pounds. At a certain point of exhaustion or self-disgust (it was never clear to him when this would occur), he would stop bingeing and begin to eat healthfully, but he would also begin exercising in what was almost a panic-stricken manner. One hour of swimming preceded ten miles of fast-paced jogging. A strenuous workout ritual was what he had to look forward to when he returned home from work. If John was lax in any of these regimes, he became severely self-critical, anxious, and was plagued with thoughts of gaining weight. The exercise for John was as drastic a purge as vomiting was for the women previously mentioned.

HOW IT BEGINS—"IT WON'T HAPPEN TO ME"

No one who decides to control weight by vomiting, laxative use, or any other forms of purging ever believes that she will end up in an out-of-control cycle of bingeing and purging. In fact, bulimia always starts out as a way of being *in* control—in control of food, of weight, of one's size, of one's image.

"I didn't think it was really such a bad thing," said Rachel, 38 and twenty years bulimic, of her first years of bingeing and purging. "At that time, I'd throw up about once or twice a month, when I decided I didn't want to keep down what I'd eaten. I figured other people smoked, or drank, or did drugs. I didn't do any of those things; so I figured they all had their thing, this was mine."

But what happened to Rachel was fairly typical. Knowing she could vomit provided the excuse to give in to the urge to eat more and more often, till she was caught up in a desperate cycle of bingeing and purging that reached its current twice-daily frequency.

No matter the method, purging provides the perfect solution for the bulimic. It allows her to continue to eat not merely to satisfy physical hunger but more importantly to meet emotional needs. An addictive cycle develops in which she relies on the binge and purge as a part of her daily life. The cycle cannot be stopped easily.

WHO IS VULNERABLE

Bulimia usually starts in adolescence or young adulthood, although recently the age of onset is occurring in girls as young as 11 or 12 and in women in their 40s and 50s. The binge-purge cycle often begins at transition points of independence (such as leaving for college, moving away from home, getting married) when stress is high and there are no other outlets for emotional conflict and tension. Another common precipitant to the bingeing and purging cycle is the breakup of a relationship with a boyfriend or spouse.

Bulimics tend to be people who do not feel secure about their own self-worth. They feel dependent on others for approval and appreciation and rely on others' judgments to determine their worthiness. As a result, they tend to be conforming and pleasing, hiding anger, upset, or other negative feelings from themselves and others.

For the bulimic, food becomes an outlet for all the feelings and conflicts that she cannot expose. The person who is vulnerable is one who doesn't utilize other ways to express her inner turmoil. The bulimia thus serves a function of blocking or letting out feelings that are experienced as unacceptable.

About 90 to 95 percent of bulimics are women. However, it is possible that there are more men who are bulimic but they are less likely to seek treatment. Men who engage in vigorous athletics, such as marathon running or strenuous workouts to control their weight, may be eating disordered. When exercise has become a way to compensate for weight gain from bingeing, and a cycle of overeating and exercising becomes a way of dealing with stress, an eating disorder has developed. However, given that exercising is not usually in and of itself worrisome (whereas vomiting is), women fill the treatment rooms.

HOW THE DISORDER PROGRESSES

What starts out as an attempt to control one's body and weight quickly becomes behavior that is out of control. Initially, turning to food actually works to make the bulimic feel calmer and less under pressure when she is upset. Because it works, the bulimia becomes entrenched as a way of coping with uncomfortable emotional states.

The bulimic thinks more and more about eating and purging. She begins to structure her day around when she'll eat, what she'll eat, how she can get rid of the calories. The bulimia inevitably takes on a life of its own and the person no longer feels that she is choosing to binge or vomit but that the binge-purge cycle has taken over her life.

Louisa, 18, talked tearfully of trying to get through the days at college struggling with bulimia:

> Every day I wake up and say I'm going to be "good" today. Usually I make it until dinner without bingeing or getting sick, but the evenings are always the worst. Sometimes I actually make it to bed—but then I lie there not being able to sleep. I keep thinking if I just ate a little it would put me to sleep. Sometimes I'll toss and turn till 3:00 or 4:00 A.M., but I always

end up giving in and eating my roommate's food or going to the candy machines in our dorm. Even if I only eat one thing, like a muffin or one candy bar, I have to throw it up or it will sit in my stomach and I can't sleep. What kills me is that every day for three years I've been doing this—starting out "good" and then blowing it every night. Do you know how that makes me feel? I feel like something crazy is happening to me. Am I going to spend the rest of my life fighting with this thing?

Another woman in her 30s, Annie, told us of a tormented struggle to stop the bingeing and get the bulimia out of her life:

> I feel like a prisoner in my own life. I can't have *one* thing in the refrigerator or I know when I come home from work I'll eat it. One night all I had in the refrigerator was one onion. The refrigerator was completely bare except for this stupid onion. I had already eaten dinner and had vowed not to eat anything more but this onion kept haunting me. Finally at midnight I gave in and sautéed it with some oil I had. That was it—I had blown it. After that I ordered in $30 worth of Chinese food. That rotten onion was the start of a three-hour binge.

Other women describe putting Ajax on food that they don't want to eat, dumping food in the garbage, having parents or roommates hide or lock up food. This is always to no avail. Food is washed, dug up from under the trash, or found no matter where the hiding place is. The struggle not to binge is as profound as the struggle for any addict trying to kick a habit.

It is a common experience for a bulimic to start the day with the vow, "Not today. Today I won't binge." Such vows are well-meaning but ignore the complexities of the bulimic's relationship to food and how great the emotional need is for food. As soon as the promise is made, all she can think about is food, and the temptation to binge is heightened.

The bulimic caught in the struggle with food often doesn't

realize that she has a treatable disorder. She thinks it is a personal failing, and lives with the torture of self-contempt. Unlike the anorexic, the bulimic *does* acknowledge she's hurting herself. She admits to her psychological distress and often knows of the physiological consequences of her behavior. Medical complications can include fatigue, sore throats, ulcerated esophagi, tooth decay, and, even worse, heart disturbances due to potassium depletion. But even when the bulimic is aware of these complications, she does not use them as motivators to change. Instead these problems are seen as proof that she is a terrible person. "Look at what I'm doing to myself" we frequently hear. "I'm slowly killing myself and I won't even stop."

Complications that lead to death are less common in bulimia, but if treatment is not pursued, bulimia can become a lifelong progressive disorder in which more and more of the person's daily activities and thoughts are oriented around food. However, because the bulimic does know something is wrong, over time she is more likely than her anorexic "sister" to seek help to change her behavior.

Compulsive Overeating

Compulsive overeating is characterized by uncontrollable eating followed by guilt and feelings of shame about the behavior and consequent weight gain. Dieting is mistakenly seen as the solution and is undertaken with strenuous effort. Feelings of deprivation set in because the dieting is approached in a rigid manner. The feelings of deprivation soon give way to a veering from the diet and the consequent despair over "blowing it" results in a return to the compulsive eating. The problem becomes cyclical and never ending because the dieting misses the point.

Compulsive overeating is a psychological disorder in which food is used unknowingly to cope with stress, emotional conflicts and daily problems. Whether overeating or dieting, the compulsive overeater is still engaged in a struggle with food.

ESSENTIAL FEATURES OF COMPULSIVE OVEREATING

- Episodic binge eating accompanied by an awareness that the eating pattern is abnormal.
- Fear of not being able to stop eating voluntarily.
- Depressed mood.
- Self-deprecating thoughts following the binges.

THE RELATIONSHIP BETWEEN COMPULSIVE OVEREATING AND OBESITY

Compulsive overeating is often confused with obesity. However, one does not necessarily imply the other. Obesity is a term used when someone weighs more than 25 percent above their expected normal body weight. A compulsive overeater may or may not be obese.

Obesity is a definition based on weight with no reference to psychological factors, and it can result from any number of conditions that are unrelated to psychological issues. Physical impairments such as brain lesions or metabolic problems can result in obesity. Compulsive overeating, on the other hand, is a psychological problem in which someone binges as a way of coping with emotional distress. The food can soothe, block out feelings, express conflicts and emotions. But the eating is not physiologically based.

In some cultures obesity is prized and women are sent to fat houses to help them gain weight to prepare them for marriage. This kind of eating and consequent weight gain has no relationship to compulsive overeating.

For the compulsive overeater, eating is driven and binges are the major source of weight gain. The person feels out of control and considers her eating to be abnormal. Like bulimics, compulsive overeaters do recognize that there is something wrong.

HOW IT STARTS

Unlike anorexia and bulimia, compulsive overeating generally has a more gradual beginning. It often starts in early childhood when eating patterns are formed. Sometimes the family focuses on the food as a retreat from feelings, as a way to feel good, or as an activity to fill otherwise empty time. Eating patterns that do not create weight gain for the growing child can result in weight problems when the person stops growing. When compulsive overeating starts in young adulthood, it is often at times of stress when the person feels ill-equipped to handle certain frustrations and emotions.

WHO IS VULNERABLE

As with the other eating disorders, the person who is vulnerable is the one for whom the food meets psychological needs. When someone does not have other tools or resources to deal with stressful situations, then food may be used as a way of coping.

Unlike bulimia and anorexia, there is a high proportion of male overeaters. Treatment is sought by men and women alike. It is a common clinical observation that compulsive overeating runs in families. People who are vulnerable often come from families in which there is an overemphasis on food and how much someone eats.

"In my family, how much you appreciated a dinner was measured by how much you ate. Whether you actually felt hungry never mattered," said one compulsive overeater. Another woman told us, "Whether I cared about starving children or hurting my mother's feelings were the incentives to eat. No one seemed to pay attention to appetite."

HOW THE DISORDER PROGRESSES

Compulsive overeating is often a chronic syndrome that remains with someone for his or her life. The psychological torment involved in this disorder can also be combined with physiological complications from poor dietary habits and consequent weight gain. Physical problems can include such difficulties as heart ailments, mobility problems, or diabetes.

The compulsive overeater is more concerned about weight gain than the physical toll on her health. The more fearful or disgusted she becomes, the more stringently she tries to diet. This dieting and the subsequent feeling of deprivation are what lead to the next binge and she suffers tormenting feelings of powerlessness as the cycle begins again.

Like a bulimic, the compulsive overeater has usually tried to stop in every way possible. Often the attempt at control is rigorous dieting and living by a system of absolutes. This inflexible system leaves no room for deviation. When the compulsive overeater goes off a self-imposed diet, the rigidity collapses and she feels all is lost. The feelings of guilt, shame, and failure that follow are the same that plague bulimics.

Diets and weight loss procedures may help intermittently, but in the long run, if they don't touch the emotional reasons for bingeing, they will not work. In fact, stringent dieting is the first step toward the binge. The experience of deprivation is the precursor to wanting food. There is no better way to create a craving than through deprivation. A pattern of bingeing and dieting can go on indefinitely when dieting is erroneously seen as the only solution to the problem.

Unfortunately, compulsive overeating is not yet taken seriously enough in our culture. The tragic view of compulsive overeaters is that they are lazy and gluttonous, or, at best, lacking in willpower or self-control. Thus instead of being treated as though they have a serious problem, they are pushed into diet centers, spas, or "fat farms" where the focus on food and diet overlooks the psychological aspects of this disorder. Compulsive overeating is as serious a problem as bulimia or anorexia in terms of the toll it takes on someone's life, and it should be treated as such.

Sharon, a 24-year-old compulsive overeater, shared her distraught feelings with us:

> I keep going to different eating disorder groups and facilities, and it's clear I don't belong there. I don't throw up, I'm not too thin, I'm not a perfectionist about my size and looks. Then when I try going to a diet group like Weight Watchers it's clear I don't belong there either. It's not simply a matter of dieting

for me. I know how to diet. I don't know how to stop the binges. It seems wherever I go I have the wrong problem. I can't even get this right.

Without the obviously strange and damaging behavior of vomiting, the compulsive overeater and those around her are less likely to identify her problem as serious. It often seems to her and others that the problem is one of too big an appetite or a stubborn lack of self-control. This mislabeling of the problem can keep the cycle going for years. Only when psychological factors are considered along with a healthy diet can behavior change be sustained.

WHAT YOU CAN OBSERVE—AND WHAT YOU CAN'T

This chapter has focused on illuminating the observable aspects of eating disorders. Many people do not fit neatly into one category or the other. Some people exhibit traits from more than one category. Other people may change their behavior over time; so, for example, they start out with symptoms that typify the anorexic and move into behaviors that are more characteristic of the bulimic.

In many situations serious eating problems go on far too long without notice. The following checklists will help you identify a situation that deserves your attention. The importance of educating yourself and having a clearer picture of what you are observing is not to categorize the person, but to have the information you will need to deal effectively with the situation.

The checklists describe signs of the three eating disorders that may be visible to the outside observer. These lists are not all-inclusive of every symptom but instead focus on what you can see and pay attention to. Check the signs that you've seen under each category. It is not important that you decide which eating disorder; just note what it is that you see. In some cases, the problem will be strikingly clear. In others, this information can be used to help a professional make a diagnostic determination. We will refer back to the information from these checklists in later chapters.

• • • •

CHECKLIST FOR VISIBLE CHARACTERISTICS OF ANOREXIA

Behavioral Signs

___ Signs of restricted eating (unusually low intake of food) such as severe diets or fasting.

___ Odd food rituals such as counting bites of food, cutting food into tiny pieces, or preparing food for others while refusing to eat.

___ Intense fear of becoming fat, regardless of low weight.

___ Fear of food and situations where food may be present.

___ Rigid exercise regimes.

___ Dressing in layers to hide weight loss.

___ Bingeing.

___ Use of laxatives, enemas, or diuretics to get rid of food.

Physiological Signs

___ Weight loss (often in a short period of time).

___ Cessation of menstruation without physiological cause.

___ Paleness.

___ Complaints of feeling cold.

___ Dizziness and fainting spells.

Attitude Shifts

___ Mood shifts.

___ Perfectionistic attitude.
___ Insecurities about her capabilities regardless of actual performance.
___ Feelings of self-worth are determined by what is or is not eaten.
___ Withdrawal from people.

CHECKLIST FOR VISIBLE CHARACTERISTICS OF BULIMIA

Behavioral Signs

___ Bingeing.
___ Secretive eating, evidenced by missing food.
___ Preoccupation with and constant talk about food and/or weight.
___ The avoidance of restaurants, planned meals, or social events if food is present.
___ Self-disparagement when too much has been eaten.
___ Bathroom visits after meals.
___ Vomiting, laxative abuse, or fasting.
___ The use of diet pills.
___ Rigid and harsh exercise regimes.
___ Fear of being fat, regardless of weight.

Physiological Signs

___ Swollen glands, puffiness in the cheeks, or broken blood vessels under the eyes.
___ Complaints of sore throats.
___ Complaints of fatigue and muscle ache.
___ Unexplained tooth decay.
___ Frequent weight fluctuations, often within a 10–15 pound range.

Attitude Shifts

___ Mood shifts that include depression, sadness, guilt, and self-hate.
___ Severe self-criticism.
___ The need for approval (including yours) to feel good about herself.
___ Self-worth determined by weight.

♦ ♦ ♦ ♦

CHECKLIST FOR CHARACTERISTICS OF COMPULSIVE OVEREATING

Behavioral Signs

___ Bingeing.
___ Restriction of activities because of embarrassment about weight.
___ Going from one diet to the next.
___ Eating little in public while maintaining a high weight.

Physiological Signs

___ Weight-related hypertension or fatigue.
___ Weight gain.

Attitude Shifts

___ Feelings about self based on weight and control of eating.
___ Fantasizing about being a better person when thin.
___ Feeling tormented by eating habits.
___ Social and professional failures attributed to weight.
___ Weight is the focus of life.

2

HIDDEN FEELINGS

The Psychological Aspects of Eating Disorders

When Joyce, a 23-year-old bulimic, came to our center for a treatment consultation, she explained her situation this way: "I have a nice apartment, a good job, a terrific boyfriend. Everything would be going okay if it weren't for the bingeing and vomiting. I've tried to make myself stop but I can't. If you could just help me get rid of the bulimia I'd be okay. I'm worried it's going to ruin my health."

Joyce was upset and confused by her eating disorder. Why was she bingeing even though it was so offensive to her? Was she lacking in willpower or strength of character? When they learned of Joyce's eating disorder, her parents were also confused. Joyce seemed to have everything going for her. What was wrong? Joyce herself didn't know. All she knew was that she couldn't stop bingeing and didn't want to be fat. She would relieve the awful fullness by vomiting. For Joyce, the reasons she was compelled to binge and vomit were as unknown to her as they were to those observing her.

WHAT'S GOING ON INSIDE?

An eating disorder is not merely a problem with food or weight. It is an attempt to use food intake and weight control to solve unseen emotional conflicts or difficulties that in fact have little to do with either food or weight. An eating disorder is *never* simply a matter of self-control. Healthier eating habits or stronger willpower are not the missing ingredients that will make the problem disappear.

Anorexia, bulimia, and compulsive overeating never exist in a vacuum. These disorders do not occur in an otherwise satisfied, productive, and emotionally healthy person. At first this may be a very hard concept to accept. Often people hope for something like a surgical procedure that will "cut out" the behavior the way a surgeon removes the offending tissues or organ. However, it is a destructive myth that the only problem is the eating behavior.

After years of failed efforts to stop bingeing and vomiting on her own, Joyce joined a support group to help her resist her strong urges to binge. After several months in this group and when she was feeling less isolated and frightened, Joyce was able to pay attention to the connection between her eating and her feelings of anxiety and discomfort:

> I have this perpetual knot in my stomach. I was never even aware of it before. It comes from worrying about "them." I don't know who "they" are—but I'm worried they will see me for what I really am, not the mature adult, but the insecure kid. It seems that when I'm feeling the most shaky about myself is when I binge.

No amount of praise or material reward could convince Joyce of her value for long. She was driven to prove herself all the time, monitoring her words and behavior in nearly all circumstances. Her self-consciousness was ever present. The more anxious or self-doubting she became, the harder she would work to prove herself. Bingeing and vomiting helped her feel some relief from her vigilance; it was an attempt to make herself feel better.

Jill, a 17-year-old anorexic, describes her experience:

> When I was starving myself, all I felt was that I *had* to. There was no rhyme or reason to it. You could not have convinced me it had anything to do with something emotional or psychological. It took time for me to see how frightened I was and how I had to feel in absolute control. It seems strange now, even a little pathetic, but my eating was all I could control: I felt I was more powerful than anyone when I wasn't eating. What a peculiar way to feel competent.

Is She Trying to Hurt Herself?

"But it's so destructive. Is she trying to hurt herself?" Joyce's mother wanted to know. The question is a common one. Eating disorders are destructive. They take a great toll, emotionally and physically. But this is not by design. Only when you understand the ways in which an eating disorder is someone's attempt to feel better about herself or to help her function in a world that feels intimidating can you see that the destructiveness is a by-product of the problem, not an intent. In fact, the self-destructiveness of compulsive overeating and bulimia causes the individual great anguish and is often a motivator to stop.

"Tell me *again* about the side effects and risks of death," requested a bulimic patient. "Maybe if I can really focus on how I am hurting myself, I can finally stop."

With another patient, it took years of intensive therapy for her to see and accept that her weight was part of a solution to an emotional problem. "I always thought the weight was the obstacle. It was what kept me from a happy life. Indeed, at 280 pounds, I and everyone else thought I was just out to kill myself—a slow suicide. It is only recently that I've begun to see that my deeper terror is that of feeling close to people—I built a natural barrier. No wonder every time I lost weight I ran right back to food."

In anorexia the destructiveness is flatly denied. Even on the brink of death, the anorexic sees her starving as essential to her sense of competence and self-esteem. It feels necessary to life, even as it kills.

In every eating disorder, it is only when the person is able to find healthier means of taking care of herself and generating internal sources of self-esteem that she can give up the attempts at coping that have, ironically and tragically, led to further emotional and physical damage. Only by understanding the protective and adaptive functions of these behaviors can *you* begin to appreciate why it may be so hard for someone to just "give it up."

An Eating Disorder Is an External Solution to Inner Turmoil

A focus on body size is a way to convert a worry about something inside to something outside. For example, if the concern "Am I good enough?" becomes "Am I thin enough?" the sufferer creates an external and measurable scale of her self-worth that offers her a less painful and more comprehensible way to cope with her fears.

Jennie, a 20-year-old overweight college student who was very pretty in spite of 60 excess pounds, describes the phenomenon this way:

> I wonder about why I can't lose the weight. Sometimes I think I stay fat because everything that is wrong in my life can be attributed to that. This way if someone doesn't like me, I can always blame it on my weight.

Not as observable as Jennie's weight was her fragile self-esteem. With or without excess weight, Jennie felt herself to be unlovable and undesirable. By focusing on the weight as the source of all discomfort, she could leave untouched the confusing and tumultuous feelings inside of her. She had an excuse for avoiding the social situations in which she felt timid and inept, and she could attribute any disappointment or hurt to her weight. Being 60 pounds lighter risked the hurts without the ready explanation.

Allison, a 15-year-old bulimic, describes what food does for her:

> I start to feel a terror, like a big, black cloud that creeps up. My thoughts start to race so fast I don't know what they are. Then I go for the food. The food calms me, distracts me. Even though I'm eating frantically and I don't taste a bite, the terror subsides. Slowly I'm back in a warm, familiar space where everything is blocked out but me and the food.

Betty, a 30-year-old bulimic, began to discover that the eating disorder was more about feeling secure than about food:

> It started to dawn on me that the bingeing and purging weren't entirely about my size and weight and then I noticed a certain pattern. When I was with a man, I was not bingeing. If someone was sleeping in my bed at night there was no urge to binge. It wasn't just that I couldn't binge because someone was there, but that the urge was gone! I noticed this when I started keeping a journal of my feelings and experiences, and it floored me! I feel so safe and secure with a man, almost any man, that I have no desire to eat. It's bizarre to me that I can feel secure with a stranger.

An Eating Disorder Is a Form of Substance Abuse

In Betty's case, she was able to substitute a man for the food in order to calm her anxiety. She experienced a man as a warm, soothing body rather than as a complex human being to interact with. In this way a man was like a substance rather than a person. Therefore, be it a man or a binge, Betty was relying on an external substance to alleviate her inner distress. When used for emotional purposes, food functions similarly to a drug or alcohol: It provides escape.

As time goes on, food replaces people more and more in the world of the sufferer, and the isolation increases.

Said one 19-year-old coed who would binge and vomit several times nightly:

> It got to be so that I would rather spend a Saturday night eating than with my friends. Being with people felt superficial. I was just killing time till I could go home and eat. I'd be carrying on a perfectly normal conversation but in the back of my mind, all I'd be thinking about was all the food I could eat as soon as I left. I knew something was wrong. I hated that food was so important, but I was trapped. I couldn't get the thoughts of food out of my head and I didn't know any way out.

She May Also Be Depressed

Many people with eating disorders grapple with low moods, low energy levels, and feelings of despondency and sadness.

In some cases, the intensity of the mood and the seriousness of associated behaviors, such as severe sleep problems, lack of interest in life, and constant self-deprecating thoughts indicate the presence of a clinical depression.

Depression is usually associated with feelings of helplessness, ineffectiveness, loss of control, and/or unexpressed anger. The relationship between feeling depressed and eating disorders is a complicated one. Because bulimics and compulsive overeaters often feel out of control, feeling depressed can be a frequent by-product of an eating disorder. After all, how would you feel if you repeatedly promised yourself to stop some destructive, disruptive behavior and failed over and over again?

In many people, depression and mood swings are the result of the disordered eating itself. Erratic and restrictive food intake can lead to internal chemical imbalances that can wreak havoc with mood.

When this is the case, the mood swings and depressed feelings will be alleviated by a normal diet. But for some proportion of sufferers, the syndrome or illness of depression has preceded the eating disorder and may be physiologically based. The relationship between eating disorders and depression is the subject of much current research. Because the research is new, the results are not conclusive, but they indicate that some people seem to have depressions of a biological nature. What proportion of the population this involves is still unclear. In these cases, the eating disorder may be the attempt to alleviate or anesthetize against the depression to make it bearable. The eating disorder may well be someone's attempt at self-medication.

Sara spoke of her periods of extreme depression:

> These waves of lethargy and dullness would come over me. The day before I'd be fine, but then I would wake up and feel such utter hopelessness and despair that there would be no point in going to work or seeing friends. What seemed to offer pleasure yesterday looked bleak and uninviting today. I couldn't move and I'd feel horrible about myself. I don't know what makes me feel like this. But once I do, it goes on for weeks and there is nothing I want to do but eat. And then it lifts—as mysteriously as it began—leaving me 10 to 20 pounds heavier.

Sara's depressions began years before the bingeing became a part of her life. She had a history of depressive episodes, but as a child her depression manifested itself through sleep disturbances and crying spells. When Sara reached 11 or 12, she found that eating alone in her room seemed to comfort and calm her. Although she didn't know it, Sara's use of food was an attempt at medicating herself for depression that no one knew existed. What started out as a naive attempt to deal with her depressive state quickly developed into bulimia.

Among the people for whom depression is associated with bulimia, antidepressants can be a helpful aspect of treatment. In Chapter 6, we discuss the use of medication and its treatment implications.

An Eating Disorder Is an Emotional Anesthetic

Whether or not she is clinically depressed, someone with an eating disorder always has a great deal of trouble acknowledging, accepting, and enduring many of her own feelings. Sometimes these are feelings that can be considered negative like anger or disappointment. Sometimes they are the more tender emotions like affection, longing, and dependence that cause problems. Sometimes conflictual feelings are the difficult ones, like wanting to be grown-up and remain a child at the same time. Feelings can be, and often are, intense for the eating-disordered person, who fears being overwhelmed by them or, worse still, overwhelming others with them. The fear of her feelings then exacerbates the problem, leading the person to panic and rush to food.

Lyla, 25, ten years bulimic and now in treatment, talks about her use of food in this way:

> Sometimes my head feels like it's going to explode. I can't stop thinking about how I should have done something differently or how I blew a relationship because of what I said. I feel like I'm going crazy with my thoughts. I can't stop it except by doing one thing—and that's eating. When I sit down with the food, all I think about is how good it tastes. Then, even when it stops tasting good, I still eat because it puts me in a daze. I can stop thinking and just numb out. It's like there's a fog around me.

BELIEVING THE PAIN WILL NEVER GO AWAY

A person with an eating disorder often believes that painful feelings will never go away on their own and nothing can be done to make them go away. "When people tell me the pain will pass or time will help, it makes me laugh," said Carin, a 36-year-old bulimic with a fifteen-year history of the disorder. "These people can't be having the same feelings I'm having. When I'm depressed it's like going into a deep, dark pit and you can't convince me there's a way out. There have been times in my life I can stay in that feeling for months. And eating is the only thing that distracts me—it is the only thing worth doing."

Carin's experience is a common one, particularly among bulimics. The fear that pain will last forever and that there is no way out makes the sufferer feel helpless and prevents her from finding solutions to alleviate the discomfort.

LEARNING TO INHIBIT FEELINGS: "THE DON'TS"

We have all been raised with "don'ts": don't do this, don't say that. Among the most common "don'ts" in the personal histories of people with eating disorders is *don't be angry* and *don't be needy*.

Young girls who ultimately grow up to struggle with eating disorders are often those who took to the classic "good girl" model—sweet, charming, perfect little girls who are unchallenging of authority, pleasing to others, and not aggressive.

Unlike their male counterparts, young girls are often encouraged to be responsible caretakers, self-sufficient, and to watch out for other people's feelings. As a result, they tend to keep a good deal of their feelings, wishes, and needs private and secret—sometimes even secret from themselves. Angry, aggressive feelings are seen as bad and unacceptable rather than the basis of healthy assertion. Because of this, young girls feel as though they're "bad" for having these feelings.

Girls who become eating disordered have often grown up believing that they should be undemanding of others. The good girl is the quiet, unseen girl who learns not to show what is bothering her. She learns her lessons well as we see in how she hides her emotions, even as her disorder progresses. She learns to feel good about herself through pleasing others, while her own "appetites" are suppressed. What other people want seems justified; what she wants is a sign of selfishness.

TROUBLESOME FEELINGS

When feelings and needs are buried, suppressed, or held back, they may remain hidden or unexpressed but they do not go away. Underneath a facade of control, optimism, or silence exist many complicated experiences that cause the eating-disordered person much distress. The following are some of the feelings and issues that cause the most common problems.

Needs for Approval/Needs for Nurturance

People with eating disorders tend to be more dependent than others. This is true even when it doesn't look that way. The eating-disordered woman relies more than most of us on other people's opinions and reflections of her to determine how she feels about herself. This is why eating-disordered people are terrified of criticism. Criticism not only means that something they do or say is not approved of by others, but it can be taken as a judgment about whether they are a good or bad person.

As Lilly, a 25-year-old recovering anorexic, told us, "If someone didn't like a dress I wore, it didn't just mean that they didn't like the dress—it meant they didn't like *me*." She had not yet learned how to give herself the support and validation she needed and thus she felt dependent on others to give her the approval that she couldn't give herself.

The eating-disordered person is not only in need of approval but inside she is "hungry" for care and affection as well. Often, she has been so attuned to everyone else's needs that her own have gotten overlooked.

Despite feelings of dependency, women with eating disorders don't want to rely on or need other people. Feeling dependent or needy leaves them feeling weak or like a failure, and is to be disowned and avoided at all costs.

For some women there is an intense fear that others will be overwhelmed by their needs and leave them, or stop loving them.

To avoid this they try to be perfect inside and out. The strain is enormous.

Amy, a 17-year-old bulimic, recently began to see how this fear affected her life.

> I know it sounds crazy and isn't logical but I genuinely feel that to be loved I must be perfect. If a guy doesn't like me I'm sure it's because I'm not thin enough, or my hair isn't nice enough, or I'm not smart enough. Then I have to work out, study harder, look better. It never occurs to me to think, "Do I like *him*?" All I can think about is that I'm not good enough.

The self-imposed demands of perfection and the fear of rejection that eating-disordered people experience interfere with the development of comfortable, intimate relationships. The dilemma is a difficult one. If someone can't reach out and allow herself to need someone else, to be vulnerable to someone else, how can she really get to know that person and let herself be known?

An experience we've heard often is that the only time someone with an eating disorder lets someone else take care of her is when she is sick. At other times, she does not feel she deserves the care and cannot allow herself to be needy. In some cases, the inability to accept care is so extreme that even when she is legitimately sick she'll deny it.

Feelings of Inadequacy

When someone grows up believing she should be stronger, more mature, more capable than her years, she meets these expectations outwardly. But her emotional, maturational development does not keep pace, and in fact can be slowed up. This leads to the experience that one is outwardly grown-up while an unacknowledged "little girl" remains hidden.

It is the little girl deep within the eating-disordered person who is frightened, who suffers the feelings of inadequacy and fears being overwhelmed. The competent facade and the exterior of independence make it hard for the onlooker to believe how young, ungrown-up, and incapable an eating-disordered person feels inside.

Abby, a 28-year-old recovering bulimic, talks about these feelings:

> At work I keep thinking that, at any minute, I'm going to be found out. Everyone thinks I'm doing a good job but I feel like I'm getting away with something and at the next step, the next task or promotion, I'll blow it. I live in terror that they'll see through me, see I really cannot do the job. It's ludicrous; I *do* do the job—why am I haunted by these fears? I feel schizophrenic—capable outside and completely inept inside.

Tanya, a recovering anorexic, recalled how such feelings haunted her high school years.

> I struggled so hard to feel I could handle it all. So instead of getting 90 on the test I had to get 100. The 90 would reveal how stupid I really was. I was terrified I would fall apart. One slipup and all would be lost. I'd be overwhelmed. I had terrible, terrible fantasies about disintegrating, blowing up into nothing. The more I could control, the more I could feel I was not going to disappear.

Food is not only used to abate the discomfort of feeling ineffectual. For bulimics and anorexics in particular, food is used as a means to feel powerful: the bulimic can defy the effects of overeating; the anorexic can defy the feelings of hunger. Both bingeing/purging and purposeful starvation can create a false sense of control. But in these disorders it is rather like Shakespeare's lady, who "doth protest too much." It is the control and defiance we see, while the inadequacy and feelings of being overwhelmed are less visible. The feelings of power are created to overcome how powerless they feel they really are.

Loneliness

"When I'm at home alone," said Jim, a compulsive overeater, "I get so lonely and it becomes a physical emptiness inside. Planning what to eat becomes an activity—it' s like planning who I'll spend time with. Food definitely is my best friend."

Jim felt he was condemned to loneliness. His self-consciousness about his weight kept him from taking part in activities and events. He thought everyone would be as disgusted at the sight of him as he himself was.

Sometimes this loneliness is like a feeling of emptiness, as though there is nothing inside. Some people experience it as "a space," "a void."

"I feel so lost," Maddie, 21 years old, said of her evenings:

> I'll be fine as long as I'm busy, but as soon as I'm home alone, nothing seems to satisfy me. I feel empty, lost, this sense of vague uneasiness. I try to read or work but I feel distracted, ungrounded. I want to be "filled up." I know my family is there and I can spend time with them, but that doesn't do it for me. Sometimes drugs or alcohol seem to take away that feeling. Other times, if I sleep with a guy that might do it too. But always whether it's food, drugs, guys, or booze, it's always temporary, leaving me feeling horrible about myself afterward. And empty still.

Loneliness, sometimes felt as boredom, is a common experience of all eating-disordered people. This feeling can occur despite the presence of other people.

"It is so peculiar," said Jerry, a 23-year-old bulimic during a group therapy session, "how lonely I can feel even when I'm not alone. It's a chilling feeling, like I'm cut off, all by myself in the world. It scares me when I feel this."

These feelings are often intensified when people are in fact alone. Some people experience being alone as though they were abandoned, left behind. Thoughts of food or exercise regimes can be company at such empty times.

Fears of People

As lonely as they are, eating-disordered people are often more comfortable with food than they are with developing meaningful relationships. Eating-disordered people have great difficulty trusting people and relationships.

Some people fear losing themselves, their own identities, in their attempts to please another person. Others fear that the other person will take over, dominating them and leaving them little room to be themselves.

Jody, a 26-year-old compulsive overeater, had trouble letting others get near her for fear she would give up control just as she always had with her mother:

> She was always doing things for me. It could be anything from changing batteries in my radio to cleaning up my room. I guess she was just taking care of me, but I felt like she was controlling everything and I came to believe I couldn't take care of myself. Now I worry about this whenever I get close to anyone else. I like being taken care of, but I quickly feel controlled. I'm so confused about this that my relationships are always in turmoil.

Many recovered compulsive overeaters have to contend with the fear of getting close to people after they have lost weight. Sexual intimacy is one aspect of emotional relatedness that can be avoided through bingeing and weight gain.

Said Cindy, a 34-year-old compulsive overeater:

> I was so afraid to let a man near me. At 200 pounds, it wasn't much of a worry. I wasn't even aware of my terror till I lost the weight and men began to notice me. Then what I had been avoiding all these years hit me. What an eye-opener—even at

120 pounds I felt inadequate and unworthy. So it wasn't the weight after all, it was me.

Anger and Aggression

As we said earlier in this chapter, girls often feel differently about their own anger and aggression than boys. Anger and aggression are very natural feelings that are the bases of healthy assertion. But with girls who grow up to develop eating disorders, angry, aggressive feelings are seen as bad and unacceptable. This often leads to difficulty managing these feelings.

Suzanne, 15, put it this way:

> I got the message loud and clear that my brothers are allowed to disagree, fight, and be aggressive. Me? I'm supposed to be polite and make sure I don't hurt anyone's feelings. I guess I learned that in spades. As soon as I feel myself to be demanding or angry, I feel terrible and selfish. With food, though, I can let this out. I tear at it and eat with my hands. If anyone ever saw me, they wouldn't believe I'm the same person. I'm in my own world and I don't care about anyone else. If they saw me they'd know how selfish I can be, how angry, how I don't really care about anyone; it would be a disaster. But at least when I'm bingeing no one gets hurt—except, I guess, me.

A child or teenager in conflict about her natural feelings of anger and aggression grows up to be an adult with equal difficulties. Only the context of her conflict broadens.

Jennifer, a 30-year-old corporate executive, describes how the requirements of her work clash head-on with her discomfort asserting herself:

> It's bizarre—here I am in charge of a whole department and I'm uncomfortable with the idea of offending anyone, making anyone mad at me. Whenever I have to assert myself, which is

> often at this job, I feel like I've done something wrong. Then I go straight for the food. Somehow when I'm eating I can forget about how badly it all makes me feel.

For the eating-disordered person who wants exclusively to be a nice, pleasing person, the experience of anger and consequent aggression can be very disruptive.

Some people manage that experience by dissociating the anger from themselves. This means that they feel like they become someone else when they binge.

Said Lettie, a 19-year-old bulimic:

> It's like there is this horrible, bingeing monster inside who takes over and I can't control it. When I'm bingeing I'm like a different person. I'll be nasty and not care about others. Usually I'm a very nice person—too nice. Usually I'm the one who takes care of everyone else first and my own needs and feelings come last.

Other people have described this aspect of themselves as being "an ogre," a "derelict," or "it's the dark side of me." One patient suggested she was more in need of an exorcist than a therapist.

It is the "monster" that eats that represents much that feels bad, out of control, ugly, and distasteful about the sufferer. In the case of bulimics, this monster is undone by purging; in the case of anorexia, defeated by control. In either case the feeling of being in a battle with oneself is a part of daily life.

Fears of Success

For many women in our society the possibility of success and the consequent feelings of competency can generate serious conflict. It can go against the grain of the role of caretaker and puts women in a position of authority which they may unconsciously undermine.

Eating-disordered women are particularly vulnerable to such conflict. They feel guilty and undeserving when they taste success.

Lauren, 27, and a compulsive overeater, found that whenever she did well at her job as an advertising executive she would go home and binge. As she explored her experience, it became clear that bingeing was a way to sabotage her success.

> At first I feel terrific, in charge, successful, and then I begin to feel uneasy, guilty somehow. I feel like I'm defying the gods. This wasn't meant to be. I start to worry what others will think of my achievements. And humiliation creeps up on me. I'm sure they're going to be thinking I don't deserve this.

The bingeing not only numbed Lauren's uncomfortable feelings, but silently undid the success she would achieve at work.

Rachel, a 16-year-old bulimic, also struggled with the disquieting effects of achievement, but differently:

> When I do really well on an exam or with a project at school and the teacher is real pleased, I feel really good for a while. Then I begin to doubt it—my achievement and their opinion of it. I destroy it. I think they are just telling me that I did well because they feel sorry for me or because they are worried about me. I have to take it all away. Sometimes I think if I really believed I did something well the pressure to keep it up would kill me.

At these times, Rachel would come home from school and binge and vomit to calm her uneasiness.

> I'd go into a panic thinking, "Was I doing okay in school or not?" Part of me believed I was doing fine. Part of me doubted everything. It was the worst feeling—like I didn't know who I was. When I ate, though, all those feelings stopped and I could start over again—I could study, or watch TV, or talk with my

family and I'd be fine. Before that, though, I felt like I was just "losing it."

Anxiety

Anxiety is a signal. It can be a very useful tool, alerting us to situations or events that make us feel vulnerable. And with this awareness we can marshal our coping skills.

For example, if the idea of an upcoming exam makes us anxious, the tension and uneasiness can be a powerful motivator to study. Anxiety provides the opportunity to prepare for the event by anticipating the possible difficulties. Anxiety gives us the opportunity to *act* to protect ourselves in potentially difficult situations.

People with eating disorders have difficulty using anxiety as a signal to cope. Because they often feel themselves incapable of dealing with stress, the anxiety becomes a signal of impending doom, a flag that whatever is coming will be emotionally overwhelming. Anxiety is something to be gotten rid of, not listened to. Therefore the experience of anxiety is often the trigger of a binge or of a tightening of controls and intensified restriction (as in the case of anorexia). While these behaviors numb the anxiety, they do nothing to help the person prepare for or protect against the actual cause of the anxiety.

THE COMPLETE PICTURE

Because the symptoms of bingeing, vomiting, exercising, or starving can be so disruptive and frightening, it is easy to pay attention only to those behaviors. To do so, however, misses the point. The overt symptoms are just the tip of the iceberg. Beneath the surface lies a much larger piece of the picture—a complicated and complex world of feelings and experiences that are very much a part of the eating disorder. Both the visible and invisible parts need to be acknowledged in order to understand the disorders of bulimia, anorexia, and compulsive overeating.

3

RULES AND RELATIONSHIPS

The Family Context of Eating Disorders

When someone in a family develops an eating disorder, it is a sign that something is wrong—not just with the individual, but with the family as well. The eating-disordered person is not the only one under stress but may just be the only one who shows it. If someone in your family has developed the symptoms of an eating problem, it is time to listen. It is time to recognize that the person with the eating disorder is not the only one in trouble.

Families with an eating-disordered child vary tremendously. In some families everything looks okay on the surface. In others the picture is overtly chaotic, with alcoholism, drug addiction, gambling, or family violence obvious to the onlooker.

However, in all families in which there is a symptomatic child, there is a common thread: the existing rules and practices that bind the family together are not accommodating the shifting needs of the individual members.

WHAT ARE FAMILY RULES?

In every family, rules evolve to help the family function. These rules have to do with how to live together, how to express intimacy, how to disagree, and how to express needs. Which feelings and behaviors are encouraged and which are disapproved of are also dictated by the rules of the family. These rules are an attempt to provide everyone with a sense of belonging, a means of communicating, and a way of living together on a day-to-day basis.

There are many examples of family rules. The following are some that you might be familiar with: "Fighting in this house is not allowed." "The family that eats together stays together." "There are no locked doors in this house."

These rules are attempts at handling disagreement, fostering closeness, and expressing togetherness. As children grow older, flexible rules allow them to enjoy more freedom as well as assume additional responsibility. Later curfews and more privacy, for example, are balanced with more household chores. Family rules exist for parents as well. In some families, these rules can provide parents the opportunity to have a life of their own (i.e., closing bedroom doors at night or going out without their children). In other families, the rules that are established can inhibit parents' freedom (i.e., bedroom doors are always open and baby-sitters are never hired). Rules do not have to be spoken to be heard. Often they are conveyed via subtle messages that are adhered to as if they were carved in stone. A certain facial expression or physical posture can carry a great deal of meaning about what is or is not acceptable in a family.

When Rules Don't Work

In families in which someone has developed an eating disorder, those rules that originally evolved to keep the family together end up inhibiting the growth and development of the individual members of the family—children *and* parents alike.

Parents are not ill-intentioned when conveying family rules. The rules that develop are an attempt to help the family cope and get along together. Parents tend to bring the rules they learned during their own upbringing into their new families, thus perpetuating patterns of coping and relating throughout the generations. This transmission of patterns however can unwittingly perpetuate less-than-ideal rules and practices.

Janie, 18, a recovered anorexic, recalled her surprise when she noticed that her grandmother treated her mother in the same way her mother treated her:

> When we all went to visit Grandma for Christmas, her first words to my mother were, "Isn't that a bit too much makeup for you?" I'm sure this has always been going on, but I had never noticed it. My mother's face flashed anger and disappointment. I wondered if my mother realized that scene could just as easily have been of her talking to me.

In Janie's family and in the family her mother came from, one rule that was apparent was that looks are important. Another rule, or pattern of relating, was that one person had a right to comment on someone else's looks or behaviors regardless of the person's age. In both families, however, the rules resulted in an accentuated focus on looks, a feeling of being criticized, and an undermining of one's ability to decide for herself how she should look.

In both families, these rules needed to be reevaluated, but it wasn't until Janie became anorexic and therapy was started that anyone imagined the family rules were taking such a serious toll.

When someone develops a symptom such as an eating disorder, it is that person's own way of fighting to evoke change. The person, however, is not someone who can fight openly; she is not a rebel. Thus her fight is subtle and disguised. When the family can understand an eating disorder as a sign to question family rules and patterns, the real problems have hope of resolution. Families that can adapt to the changing needs of their family members by reevaluating the rules have a better chance of the eating disorder taking a transient, short-lived course as opposed to becoming embedded in both the individual's and family's life. However, when the solution involves an attempt to control the eating behavior, the eating disorder always gets worse.

WHEN RULES AFFECT FEELINGS

Pearl Greene, the mother of an anorexic daughter, was an 8-year-old child when her own mother developed cancer. Her mother spent many years bedridden as Pearl, the only daughter, tended to her. Pearl's childhood was lost to her mother's illness, and as Pearl entered her teenage years without the freedom to date or enjoy after-school activities like the other teenagers, her anger and resentment understandably grew. At night, alone in bed and tearful, Pearl would wish that her mother would die so she could have her own life. When Pearl was 15, her "wish" was granted—but horror, not relief, followed. Maybe her mother had known of Pearl's anger. Maybe it killed her. Pearl's mother's death did not release her—it haunted her even through her own marriage and family life. In the Greene family, Pearl made it clear that anger was to be avoided at all cost.

Pearl's experience with death and her fear of the consequences of anger pervaded her experiences with others. The effects of Pearl's experience influenced her daughter Emily, a 16-year-old high school student who is now recovering from anorexia.

Emily describes it this way:

> Whenever I would get angry at my father and start to say anything, my mother would put her hand over her heart like she was warning me. This would stop me cold. I'd just stop what I was saying and leave. But I always felt angry and frustrated. The first time my mother didn't do that was when I was in the hospital and my parents thought I might die because I was so thin. Then my mother was more frightened about my dying than my getting angry.

When family rules inhibit the experience or expression of feelings, the opportunities to accept and resolve these feelings are thwarted. Pent-up feelings may result in explosive episodes, in which release comes in a torrent of emotions that are uncontrollable and usually not productive. Pent-up feelings also often lead to physical illnesses, including stomach problems, back pain, colitis, and asthma. Or, they may lead to psychological symptoms as expressed in an eating disorder. When symptoms are the result of unexpressed feelings, one not only misses the chance to learn how to accept emotions and use them constructively, but one can continue believing that everyone will respond to feelings like people at home did. Rules about feelings are often problematic in families with an eating disorder. The areas of trouble include the following:

Expression of Feelings: "You're Going to Kill Your Father If You Say That"

In the Greene family, Pearl had made it clear that anger was to be avoided. This was not an arbitrary rule but an attempt on Pearl's part to keep the family together. From her own experience, she learned that anger was a powerful and dangerous emotion. The "rule" to not get angry was her way to avoid replicating in her new family what she believed happened in her original family. The problem with this rule was that while it was well-intentioned, it left all the members of the family restricted in their expression of a wide range of feelings. In part, Emily's anorexia provided a way to express upset in a family that tried so hard to keep unpleasant emotions buried.

The direct experience and expression of intense feelings such as anger, resentment, disappointment, jealousy, sadness, and loss are necessary for healthy functioning. In many eating-disordered families there is a rule, sometimes subtle, sometimes not, that these unpleasant feelings are to be avoided. Pearl thought anger could be hurtful. Others may have come from families in which feelings actually did get out of control and resulted in violence. Certainly, rules inhibiting emotional expression would feel like life-protecting devices in this case. For some people expressing painful feelings is a sign of weakness. In any of these situations, when rules develop that stop the natural expression of feelings, finding effective and modulated means of expressing them seem impossible.

Kevin Dwyer, 42, had grown up in a strict Irish-Catholic family. In his family, one unquestionably respected one's elders. Most displays of emotion were strongly discouraged. His own upbringing influenced how he raised his daughter Maureen. Maureen describes it this way:

> My mother died when I was 6 years old and my father remarried when I was 10. As soon as he married my stepmother, they both insisted I call her Mom. I didn't want to, but they forced me to. All the pictures of my mother were taken off the living room walls. I didn't mind that so much, but then my father made me put away all the pictures of my mother that I had in my bedroom. I'd have to sneak away to look at them. Sometimes I'd ask questions about my mother and my father would give me a dirty look and say, "You only have one mother, ask her." When I got older, I really wanted to know things about her, particularly in what ways I was like her. But my father would never tell me. I had a ritual in those days. I would buy lots of sweets and gather all the pictures I had of my mother, close my bedroom door, eat, and look at them.

Kevin Dwyer was not trying to be mean to his daughter. It was just that he himself had never expressed his own feelings of sadness and loss as a child. Now as an adult, faced with the traumatic loss of his wife, he turned to the familiar rules of his family: "Pull it together," "Don't think about it," and certainly "Don't let it show."

Naturally, Maureen abided by these same unspoken rules, and food became the only safe outlet for her unexpressed feelings about her mother. Eating helped her to ease her loneliness and sadness.

Expression of Conflict: "Our Family Never Fights"

One of the reasons that families avoid direct expression of intense feelings is that they fear conflict among family members. If people say what they feel, they may not agree with each other and tension, arguing, and conflict will result. To some, conflict calls into question the family's closeness; it is interpreted to mean that people do not love one another. Complaining or disagreeing threatens the bonds of the family. Therefore a high value is placed on everyone getting along well. The rule, then, often unspoken, is that one doesn't behave in ways that may cause conflict.

Such a rule, designed to keep the family close, may have consequences for the children. When there is no acceptable way to disagree and be different, there is no way for someone to learn to trust and value her own experiences.

Katherine, 18, once 82 pounds, has been in therapy for three years and is now at a normal weight. She describes a history typical to many anorexics:

> I was always the good one around the house. My room was never messy. I did well in school. I always helped my mother. I know my parents hated fighting. If my brother or I ever raised our voices my mother would say, "Sh-h, now say it in a nice tone." How can you be angry in a nice tone?
>
> I went on being the good child and the good student. I never disobeyed.
>
> It was in my sophomore year in high school that I began dieting after gaining weight during the summer. Dieting and losing weight was a real high for me. After I'd lost a lot of weight, my mother got upset and tried to make me eat. But she couldn't.
>
> I didn't know it then, but now I realize that my not eating made me powerful. It was really me fighting with my mother.

The reasons to avoid fighting were different for Joan and Jim Ross. Jim grew up watching his father and older brother fight constantly. Often the fighting got out of control and on one occasion Jim's father knocked Jim's brother unconscious. Another time, Jim's brother was so mad that he threatened to kill everyone in the house. Jim, at age 10, believed he might do it. Jim grew up fearful that anger could be dangerous. When he married Joan and had children, his feelings about conflict didn't change.

Joan had reasons of her own for wanting a peaceful household. Joan's parents never fought. They prided themselves on this quality and taught Joan that a couple with a good marriage didn't disagree. In the Ross family the rule "no disagreements" was strictly adhered to.

For Pam, the Rosses' bulimic 17-year-old daughter, this presented an agonizing dilemma. At an eating-disorder group, she asked:

> What can I do? It's a losing battle. All my friends stay out and go to parties. I want to be a part of it, but my folks get upset. They want me to be home early and always stick around for Sunday—Family Day, they call it. They have this idea that we're all supposed to be so close. I love my parents but sometimes what they want is too much. Whenever I get pissed off at them and their ridiculous ideas, they get incredibly upset. My mother cries; my father looks hurt and says, "Let's just forget all this and have a nice evening." I want to scream—but what I do instead is eat. It's the only thing that keeps me from fighting with them—and fighting is just too upsetting. I'm so miserable about this whole thing.

As Pam's eating disorder increased, the family became more and more embroiled in Pam's eating problem. However, as the focus shifted to food, Pam's struggle to disagree with her parents (a common teenage pastime) was obscured. Little by little Pam stopped fighting with her parents about going out. As long as the struggle remained in the arena of eating, there was less and less hope of resolution of the other issues regarding Pam's attempts to grow up.

Assuming and Ascribing Feelings: "You Must Be Hungry"

When open communication is inhibited, family members are left to guess or assume what the others feel. When assumptions about feelings are made, children grow up without the opportunity to learn about, trust and communicate their own feelings.

Elaine Peters, now 42, came from a family in which every birthday and holiday was celebrated. Forgetting family members' birthdays meant you weren't thinking about them either because you were angry at them or they didn't mean much to you. If someone forgot Elaine's birthday, she was hurt and her family accepted her feelings as legitimate.

Her husband Richard, 44, on the other hand, came from a family that rarely celebrated birthdays or made much of holidays. In his family, the "rule" was to buy a gift for someone when one felt like buying something or when one saw something special that someone else would want. His family believed birthdays were artificially imposed occasions that did not warrant special attention or gift buying.

The first year that they were married, Elaine's birthday came and went without Richard saying a thing. Elaine was hurt and upset. To her, Richard's behavior meant that she was forgotten and unloved. She responded to Richard with angry silence. Richard, on the other hand, did not know why Elaine was treating him this way, and he responded by emotionally withdrawing. His withdrawal was further proof to Elaine that he didn't care enough about her, and their frustrating interaction continued.

Neither Elaine nor Richard asked what the other was feeling. Elaine assumed she knew what Richard's behavior meant because of what it would have meant in her own family. Richard didn't ask because in his family it was considered pushy to ask people what they felt—if they wanted you to know, they'd tell you. By operating under rules that they were accustomed to in their own families, Elaine and Richard could only see the situation as their original families would have seen it. Each was stuck in his or her own perspective, so that they could not move on to develop new rules that would be more satisfying for both of them. The birthday situation finally erupted into an angry fight. The fight ended when Richard resolved to remember all future holidays and birthdays. However, while the gift-giving aspect of the problem was solved, both Richard and Elaine continued to avoid asking what the other person was feeling. A pattern of guessing or assuming, rather than asking about what someone was feeling, persisted as a family norm—and often one or the other was wrong.

In families where feelings are not directly expressed but instead assumed, the die is cast for children who enter into these families. They, too, have feelings ascribed to them that they don't necessarily experience.

Kerry, 22 and bulimic, brought this issue up in her support group:

> My parents spent my childhood telling me what *they* thought I was feeling instead of ever asking. They weren't trying to be mean or anything. It's just that they'd say things like, "You'd like to go to Aunt Jean's on Sunday, wouldn't you?" or "You don't mind baby-sitting for your brother Friday night," or "I know you must be hungry." I'd always know from their questions what they'd want me to say and I'd answer that way—I hated to let them down. I also think I believed that *they* really knew what I wanted better than I did. Even today I expect people will know what I want without my having to say so. It's ironic—now when people ask me what I feel or want, I resent their not knowing.

Kerry was responded to with much head nodding in the group. "I've been talking a lot about this in therapy," a 24-year-old bulimic woman said:

> I too was raised by parents who always thought they knew what I was thinking. I was a quiet kid and I remember if I wasn't bubbly and talkative about guys and school (like my sister Chrissie), my mother would think I was mad at her. "What are you so angry at?" she'd ask. "What did I do now?" Then I would get mad at her because her questions were so annoying. She made me wonder if I was angry at her when I was quiet. It got so that at times I didn't know what I was feeling. Even now, my insides seem like a puzzle—sometimes I can't figure out what it is I'm feeling. I know my mother didn't mean to be cruel but the effect was cruel. I've ended up so unsure of myself.

Growing up in a family where feelings are inhibited instead of openly expressed can lead to assuming and ascribing feelings in later relationships. Lila, a 24-year-old bulimic woman, married to Charles, 29, talked about how this was so in her marriage:

> When I was growing up, no one in my family would ever say if he or she felt angry. If I even got mildly angry about something my folks would get upset. They feared my being angry meant that they weren't being good parents. When I got angry I'd end up feeling guilty. I learned to act as though I felt fine no matter what was going on inside me.
>
> Now, as an adult, I don't even know if I'm angry half the time—and if I am, I certainly can't say it.
>
> After I started therapy for bulimia, though, my therapist helped me see that at times I do get angry at Charles. But instead of telling him that I'm mad, I'll think he's the one who's upset and I'll ask him, "What's wrong?" He'll say nothing. Then I keep asking him over and over what he's upset about. Pretty soon, he is angry at me because I'm bugging him so much.

My therapist helped me see that the way I let out my own feelings is by putting them on Charles. Now, whenever I think he's angry at me, I ask myself whether that's what *I'm* feeling.

WHEN RULES DON'T SHIFT: PROBLEMS GROWING UP

Another common problem in eating-disordered families is that rules do not flexibly shift in response to family members' ages, needs, and capabilities. For children in particular, flexible rules are necessary to allow for natural dependence while encouraging increasing autonomy. This enables children to test their expanding capacities in a safe environment that allows for failure while parents are still available to help.

The transition from being the parents of young children, where watchfulness and protectiveness are necessary for the child's survival, to being the parents of adolescents, where this watchfulness should decrease, is a difficult one. It is a shift that requires parents to allow the teenager to try things on her own even when the parents know a better way. When parents are able to make this shift, the children develop an increasing sense of their own competency and ability to negotiate the demands of the outside world. When parents have difficulty shifting rules, when rules do not allow for independent behavior or are too rigid and fixed, children may fight for these changes in indirect ways. Withdrawal from the family, the use of drugs or alcohol, the refusal to eat or eating secretly are among the behaviors resorted to when a child feels helpless and controlled.

While these behaviors may allow for a feeling of independence, they do so at a high cost. They limit the child's natural and healthy capacities to grow up and achieve a life independent of her parents, and instead leave her with a destructive method of asserting herself.

When Rules Inhibit Freedom

Jenette Cuso was 16 when her mother brought her into therapy for bulimia. "She just binges all night long, Doctor. I buy food for the family and it's gone by morning. Then she's in the bathroom at all hours of the night getting rid of it."

Jenette saw the problem differently. "That may be what's upsetting you, but I'm suffocating. You never let me stay out with my friends. I have to be in at 10:00 P.M. on the weekends. All my friends stay out later. I'm always the one who has to leave the parties. You don't trust me, but you've never given me a chance."

The rules were no different for Jenette than for her younger 14- and 13-year-old sisters. Being older made no difference.

The Cusos, first-generation Italians, were fearful of what problems freedom could bring to teenagers. Drugs were rampant in Jenette's school and one of her friends had already had an abortion. The Cusos were not going to let that happen to Jenette. But Jenette did not feel protected by her parents' rules. The only thing she felt was that she was being punished—and for no reason. At night while she sat at home, feeling lonely and resentful, she took control in the only way she could. By eating and then getting rid of the food, she had freedom over what happened to her and her body at a time when she had no freedom in the rest of her life.

In anorexia, the attempt at control is much more obvious. Betty Chin's situation is an example. She never overtly objected to her parents' outings, vacations, and endless family gatherings in which she was expected to be a cheerful addition. At 17, however, she would have preferred to stay home, talk on the phone, or even do schoolwork. Sometimes she just needed time alone. If she even hinted that she didn't want to go, Mr. Chin would remind her how her 13-year-old brother and 9-year-old sister would be there too, and he insisted that the whole family be together. Once Betty stopped eating and the family became worried about upsetting her, less and less was asked of her. In the context of family rules that did not allow for the growing independence and increased freedom a 17-year-old needs, not eating became a way for Betty to say, "No. I don't always have to do what you want."

When Boundaries and Privacy Are Sacrificed

All families create boundaries to allow for privacy, independence, increased control, and a sense of separateness. Just the way people create boundaries around the land they own so no one will trespass, so are there boundaries around people. There are individual boundaries for each person and boundaries around groups of people, such as with spouses or siblings.

When the family has difficulty establishing, maintaining, and respecting boundaries, problems develop. People can feel intruded upon. One extreme yet all-too-frequent occurrence in families with eating disorders is incest, where a child's own body is not safe from intrusion. A less extreme occurrence is when a parent enters a teenager's room without permission and goes through her possessions or reads her private diary. Boundaries, especially those that have to do with privacy, also need to shift as children grow up.

Boundaries in families with eating disorders tend to be blurred. There may not be sufficient privacy, and closed doors may not be respected or even exist. In one family we met at a support group, all the doors had been removed from the children's rooms.

The intrusion may be emotional and not easy to pinpoint. As we saw in families where feelings are ascribed and not expressed, a child may not learn to be comfortable as an individual separate from her parents, with different ideas, thoughts, and feelings.

Marcia, a 24-year-old who suffered from anorexia, talked about living in her family:

> I always felt confused when I was growing up. My mother would use the word "we" whether she was talking about me or about herself. Someone would ask how I was and she would say,

"We're fine." I had trouble figuring out what were my feelings and what were hers.

One of the ways in which parents set a boundary between themselves and their children is by establishing rules. When parents make rules they are assuming a position of authority and creating a structure in the family that permits children to feel protected and dependent.

For some parents, the position of authority is difficult to assume. They want to feel close to their children and fear that if they set limits their children will get angry and not love them. This type of closeness can make it hard for the child to become independent. If a child is made to feel like the friend of a parent, rather than the child, she does not have the opportunity to grow away—to develop meaningful relationships apart from the parents.

Rachel, 24, and her mother Elise were best friends. They spent lots of time together, and there wasn't anything they couldn't tell each other. Rachel felt lucky to have a mother who was so much fun. It was only with her mother that her excessive weight did not make her feel uncomfortable about herself.

The trouble came when Rachel met a man she was interested in. She had rarely dated during college but now there was Richard, someone who was interested in her. As Rachel and Richard began to spend time together, Rachel noticed she didn't feel like calling her mother every day.

When Rachel didn't call Elise, Elise would call and complain to Rachel about her loneliness and ask if Rachel had forgotten she had a mother.

Rachel would then insist to Richard that her mother come with them on different weekend outings. Richard resented this and it led to many arguments between them.

After a few months of this, Richard ended the relationship. He was tired of having Rachel's mother so much a part of their relationship. Rachel, upset and torn between closeness to her mother and her relationship with Richard, contacted us for therapy.

Rachel realized she and her mother were and had always been

too close. There were insufficient boundaries between mother and daughter. Rachel was having trouble developing a private, independent life without feeling as though she was deserting her mother. She was beginning to suspect that her extra pounds kept her closer to home.

The worst possible sort of boundary violation with the worst consequences for the victim is incest. In the family histories of bulimic and compulsive overeating women, incest is tragically all too common.

After two years in therapy, Denise, 26 and a compulsive overeater, opened up about the abuse she suffered as a child:

> At night I'd listen for his footsteps. The house would be quiet. I'd hear the whir of the refrigerator, the hiss of the steam—and then his footsteps. He'd tell me to shove over in bed, he wanted to hold me. But he never stopped there. He said my skin was soft, I was pretty. He made me touch him. But for some reason the part that was the worst was when he kissed me. Everything else I could pretend wasn't happening to me. But the taste of his saliva, the smell of his breath, that part I could never block out.

When Denise's father would leave her room, Denise would retreat to the safety of the kitchen. There she crammed food into her mouth quickly to rid herself of the tastes in her mouth. "I felt safe then. The food numbed everything. It was a wall around me that made me feel like nothing, no one could get in. Weight became a wall too. Sixty extra pounds of fat is a hard thing to penetrate. Sometimes I imagine I'm this little person inside my big shell of a body."

Without the physical and psychological boundaries between father and daughter that should normally exist in a family to protect a child, and without her mother's help to enforce these boundaries, Denise had to resort to food and weight to obliterate the horrifying experiences her father subjected her to. The type of trauma that Denise experienced is often never revealed. Physical violations such as incest leave the victim with a sense of powerlessness that pervades her experiences with people for the rest of her life and often contributes to substance abuse (such as eating disorders) in attempt to block out and deny the impact of these traumas.

When Roles Inhibit Growth

As we mentioned in Chapter 1, eating disorders, particularly anorexia and bulimia, often develop at times of transitions—entering adolescence, going to college, moving out to live on one's own, or getting married. The child or young adult, unprepared for the adjustments that are necessary at these times, turns to food to express conflicts or quell anxiety about the impending changes.

One reason someone may be anxious and conflicted about leaving home is that she may have played a role in her family that she and other family members are hesitant to have her stop. We have found that people with eating disorders have often adopted the role of surrogate husband or wife. This is particularly true when parents have had difficulties resolving issues together as a couple. Unwittingly they pull their children into battles that are really fights between them. Or they may have given up the idea that they can have their emotional needs met by their spouse, so instead they rely more heavily on their children. Either way, when children are mediators in a marriage or have become more like a spouse than a child, it is hard for them to leave home. Children who have become like spouses worry about how lonely their parent will be when they're not there.

In one family with a 20-year-old bulimic whose mother complained bitterly about how awful the marriage was, the daughter had filled in for her father, spending most of her time with her mother. When we asked the daughter what she feared would happen if she left home, she said, "My mother would leave my father, and my father would die."

Julie, another young bulimic, spoke about her problem this way:

> My parents have always had a bad marriage. My mother told me, "My courtship was hell, my engagement was hell, and my marriage is hell." My parents never do anything together; they haven't slept in the same room for years. When they are together, they fight all the time. I don't think we've ever sat through a meal as a family without one of them screaming and then leaving the room. My father spends a lot of time with his family or at work and my mother seems so lonely. Over the years I became the one she spent her time with. I can't stand to be away from her for very long. I never go anywhere where I can't be home in an hour. I never sleep anyplace but at home. On weekends I often take her with me when I go out with my boyfriend. If I'm not there, I don't know what will happen to her.

When Julie did leave, her worst fears came true and her mother became ill. Julie spent a tormented semester at college before she dropped out to return to her ailing mother. When she returned home, she also came into treatment, where she worked hard in developing her resources, so that she could care for her mother and maintain a life of her own as well. When her mother recovered sufficiently to resume some of her own care, Julie had the strength to resist her mother's subtle but powerful inducements to remain her primary companion. After much discussion her mother agreed to see a professional counselor to help her assume responsibility for herself and work on developing a life apart from her daughter.

WHEN RULES ARE UNPREDICTABLE: CHAOTIC FAMILIES

In some families, difficulties arise because the rules are changeable, confusing, and unpredictable. As a result, the child learns to depend on herself, not on the stability of the family, and independence may come too soon, leaving the child fearful and anxious. She may turn to food to calm her anxiety—or refuse it to make herself feel stronger.

In families where the rules are chaotic or unstable, there is frequently drug or alcohol abuse. Children with eating disorders are more likely than others to have parents who abuse substances.[1] The parents' involvement with substances interferes with their ability to provide a stable family structure and consistent rules for the child.

These families often function from crisis to crisis. The household can be disorganized and many times the children are left with responsibilities that would otherwise be in the hands of the parents. A child or adolescent in such a position is left feeling inadequate. She does not have the resources or abilities to cope with all the problems that occur in filling the gaps. While she may appear to be functioning well, this is often a precocious independence and an autonomy built on sand.

It took Grace, 15, months to speak to her support group about her divorced mother's drinking problem:

> I don't know what it's going to be like when I come home from school. If she's had a "good" day, she's a lot of fun. She'll ask me how my day was, she'll suggest we make dinner together or go shopping. But if she's been drinking (which lately is more often than not) she'll have passed out on the couch with the TV blaring. Then I know if I don't shop for dinner and cook, my two younger brothers and I won't eat. Even when she wakes up, she's so groggy that it's up to me to get my brothers washed up and to bed. At around 11:00 P.M., the house is quiet and I can finally get to my homework. I'm just scared I can't keep it up. Last week I got my first C ever. This is getting to me.

What Grace didn't tell the group until two months later was how food fit in. "At night when it's quiet, when I'm doing my homework I eat. All night sometimes. But I'm scared of gaining

1. D. Herzog, "Bulimia: The secretive syndrome," *Psychosomatics* 23 (1982): 481–487.

weight so that's why I started taking laxatives. It started at 1 or 2 but now I can take 50 at a time before they work."

When substance abuse exists among parents, strong messages are communicated about experiencing and conveying feelings—in particular, that you can numb your feelings and that pain or upset will not go away on its own. The children hear a clear message: feelings are unmanageable and substances help.

WHEN RULES FOCUS ON APPEARANCE

In families in which eating disorders occur, there is a high value placed on appearance, and rules about how one looks are as powerful as rules about how one behaves.

In these families, looking good is synonymous with being worthwhile. Audrey, 24 and bulimic, described her family's focus on her looks:

> When I walk in the door to greet my parents, the first thing they say is, "Oh, you look great—you've lost a few pounds" or "Did you cut your hair? It looks shorter." The worst thing is when they won't say anything. Then I know that they think I've gained weight or don't look so good and they don't want to hurt my feelings. It's ridiculous but now if someone I'm with doesn't say I look good, I think they're being critical of me.

The importance of looking good is passed through the generations. The parents of an eating-disordered child are often very concerned themselves about how they look, their own parents having put a high value on appearances.

Often parents may not be aware of the stringent messages they are giving about food, weight, and self-control. A father was surprised that his 25-year-old daughter was bulimic. When asked about his own food habits, he said, "I do worry about my weight. I've trained myself over the years not to eat many sweets. Every night I eat half an oatmeal cookie. If it's a whole cookie, I cut it in half and wrap the other half in Saran Wrap to eat the next night. I never eat more than that half a cookie, no matter what the occasion."

His daughter could not help but criticize herself for her own lack of self-discipline. If she ate one bite more than she wanted to, she felt compelled to vomit everything she had just eaten.

Karen, a 17-year-old anorexic, spoke about her mother's preoccupation with appearance:

> My mother was always talking about weight. She was on a new diet every other week. She would be at my father to lose weight. She'd keep at him until he would go to Weight Watchers. Then the two of them would be watching everything they ate and what I ate. My mother would say, "All anyone in this family has to do is look at food and they gain weight."
>
> I recall when my brother's fiancée broke off their engagement. He was really upset and he started eating a lot. Soon he had a potbelly. Whenever my mother would see him, she'd tell him how awful he looked. She never asked him how he felt. I could see my brother feeling worse when he spent any time with my parents.
>
> My mother would comment about every pound I gained. My junior year in high school, she became even more concerned about my weight. She warned me about what happens to freshman girls in college. She said I should be ten pounds lighter than my usual weight so when I gained the ten pounds in college, I wouldn't have that college freshman look. There wasn't a day I walked in the house from school that she didn't comment on how I dressed and what I looked like.
>
> What she said about gaining weight in college really scared me. I remember starting to diet thinking I'd get a head start before I went to college. The more weight I took off, the better I felt. My mother thought so too. It got so that I was afraid that if I ate anything I'd gain weight. It was only when I started to faint that my mother realized my looking good might kill me.

Karen's mother was not ill-intentioned. She was only transmitting the rules about appearance that she had grown up with. She herself was an attractive woman, and her attractiveness was a quality for which she was often praised and admired. Her focus on looks was not meant to hurt Karen but an attempt at encouraging a quality that she thought would be helpful to her daughter.

Another reason why appearance is so highly valued in some families is that some parents feel responsible for how their child looks or behaves, responsible in a way that overrides the child's right to determine how she feels she should look or act. Consider, for example, the child who has a messy room. Some parents feel it is a negative reflection of their parenting if their child doesn't take good care of her room. The same is often the case with the child's body. In some families a messy or overweight child is seen as a sign that something is wrong with the parents, and therefore every effort is made to urge the child to lose weight. In these cases, however, the goal in mind is not merely the well-being of the child, but to reduce the uneasiness the parents feel about themselves.

CHANGING THE RULES

When someone in a family develops an eating disorder, the symptom creates stress for the family which often results in difficult situations getting worse. If rules are rigid, they usually become even more strict. If rules are chaotic, the presence of a symptom adds to the confusion.

The symptom needs to be understood as a sign that something is wrong with the rules, patterns of interactions, and communication in the family or relationship. The rules and ways of relating need to be reevaluated and changed, allowing both you and the person you care about new ways of operating in the relationship.

PART II

Confronting the Problem

4

NO MORE SECRETS

Bringing It Out in the Open

If you suspect or know that someone is eating disordered, one of the first questions you will probably ask yourself is whether you should say anything to the person you're worried about. And if you do speak to her, what should you say?

If you think someone is eating disordered, this is no time for secrets. If the person does not know you are worried about her, the first thing you must do is tell her. Silence at these times will at best continue the discomfort and at worst lead to a dangerous and serious problem being ignored. No change can occur without first breaking the silence.

PLANNING TO TALK

Bringing up the subject of an eating disorder is never an easy task, but if done with some planning and forethought, difficulties and embarrassments can be minimized. What you say can potentially influence the course of the person's recovery. You will need to anticipate how you should approach the subject, what will be said, who will say it.

This chapter will help you anticipate what will happen in the discussion and will offer effective guidelines. By planning the discussion in advance, you can ease the discomfort and anxiety you are inevitably feeling and, by being prepared, you will have the best chance of being understood.

HOW TO APPROACH THE PROBLEM

Use the following seven guidelines before speaking with the person you're concerned about:

1. *Think through who the best person is to do the talking.*

If you are a parent, decide with your husband or wife if you should both be there, or if a one-on-one conversation would work better. If the latter is the case, decide who would have an easier time talking to her without getting upset. Don't involve the rest of the family until after the child is spoken with privately.

If you are a sibling and concerned about your sister, you may want to speak with her privately or you may want your parents to do so. If your sister is a minor or you are a minor, your parents must be informed.

If you are a spouse, it is your responsibility to speak with your wife or husband. You can discuss together if anyone else needs to be told. Respect her privacy, and do not speak with friends, in-laws, or others until you speak with your spouse.

If you are a friend or roommate, you should be the person to do the talking initially. Do not go to authorities or family until you have spoken with your friend first. In a house in which there are several roommates, a house meeting can be called in which anyone affected by the problem can participate. In the latter case, only one person should initiate the discussion, so that there will be less likelihood of the person feeling attacked by everyone at once.

2. ***Pick a time to talk when you are feeling calm.*** Do not try to bring up this subject when you are angry, upset, or hurt. If you are upset, your pain may be burdensome to the other person—it may be harder for her to open up if she fears causing you even more pain. In addition, your feelings may interfere with your achieving the goals that you have in mind. Do not bring up your concerns in the middle of a fight. Accusations, confrontations, pleas to change will only result in shutting down potential lines of communication. The other person is likely to end up defending herself and will perceive your concerns as a criticism or an attack. If someone is defensive, she certainly will not be open to hearing you out at that time.

3. ***Pick a time to talk when you know you won't be interrupted.*** For example, don't start such a discussion ten minutes before you have to go to work or you will feel very pressured. This pressure can make things go badly. The time limit may discourage the other person from opening up to you because of a fear of being cut off. Both of you must know you have as much time as is needed to talk.

4. ***Consider writing down what you want to say ahead of time.*** It is inevitable that you will feel anxious or worried when you start to talk; that is natural and to be expected. By familiarizing yourself with what you want to say before you actually say it, you will be clearer when you do speak and your anxiety may be lessened. You'll also be sure to remember everything you want to say once you start talking. There are three things you will need to address in the discussion: what your worries are, how you feel, and what you would like the outcome of the discussion to be.

What Is Worrying You?

When you discuss your concerns, you need to explain why you have come to suspect a problem. You will want to be specific about what you see with regard to the eating, purging, exercising, starving, or weight-related behaviors. If you have noticed changes that affect your relationship, you will need to point these out as well. Use the information from the checklists in Chapter 1 to help you clarify what it is you see or suspect.

When you have the discussion, you are going to have to be as direct and frank as you can. For example, as hard as it is to say, "I hear you vomiting," this is much more honest than, "I think you spend a lot of time in the bathroom." If you say the latter, you are leaving the door open for the problem to get ignored or denied. The implied message is, "I really don't want to talk about this either." If you are open in your approach, you are saying, "I know this is embarrassing but I want to be of help—let's address this problem head-on for what it is."

You are going to have to be careful not to make this an indictment of what you see. Your observations should not be listed as evidence of wrongdoing, but should be discussed gently as bases for your concern. This is a subtle distinction that has to do with tone and approach but one that can make all the difference in the world.

During your talk you will have to stick to the issue and keep yourself from becoming distracted. If she changes the subject tell her you'd like to find some time to speak about these other matters, but for now you don't want to avoid the problem at hand. You should let her know that *you* know this is a hard problem to talk about but that you don't want to let the issue get sidetracked.

What Do You Feel About It?

When planning what you will say, include letting the person know what your experience is. One way to do this is to use what are called "I" statements. "I" statements are statements that focus on your own feelings and experience, not that of the other person.

Merely using the word "I" does not make for an "I" statement. "I think there's something wrong with you," and "What is the matter with you? I wonder what kind of person eats all that food and then throws up?" are *not* "I" statements. They focus on the other person and will be heard as attacking or blaming.

An "I" statement involves talking about yourself. "I've been worried about what I'm seeing. I haven't known whether to approach you or not, but I'm feeling too troubled not to say something," or "The missing food is making me really angry. I don't like walking around being so mad at you. I want to find some way of working this out." We are not suggesting you negate your own anger, frustration, or hurt. You are in an upsetting situation and will naturally have many reactions to this. However, merely venting feelings will only result in the person's becoming defensive and your being shut out. We are encouraging you to express your feelings in a way that you will be heard.

Using "I" statements does not mean you can't talk about the other person. Of course you will need to tell her why you are worried and what you perceive the problem to be. ("I've heard you vomiting," or "You keep mentioning how worried you are about your weight lately.") But it is important to avoid telling the person how you think *she* feels. For example, avoid making statements like, "You must be very angry or you wouldn't be doing this." Resist judging the other person's experience. This will decrease the possibility of the other person's feeling attacked or controlled and will increase the success of your conversation.

What Are Your Goals?

The third area that you should think through is what you would like to accomplish in this discussion. Be sure your goals are realistic and attainable.

IMPOSSIBLE GOALS

If your goal in approaching someone is to get them to stop bingeing, purging, or starving—STOP! This is an impossible task and you will fail in your attempts. You will most likely end up in a control battle and make matters worse. For any eating-disordered person, bringing the problem out in the open is a beginning stage in the process of recovery.

You cannot make a person stop her behavior, but if you are coercive you can teach her how to be more secretive and less talkative. Instead, provide support so that she is encouraged to explore what *she* wants to do about the eating disorder.

REALISTIC GOALS

OPENING THE DOORS TO TALK. You will want to let her know that she can talk with you and that you're interested in helping her. If, in your family or relationship, people tend not to open up to each other, you may need to make a special point of your availability to listen, to help, and even to make changes.

CHANGING HOW THE EATING DISORDER IS AFFECTING YOU. A realistic goal can be to change how the eating problem is interfering with your life or your relationship with her.

Some questions to ask yourself are: Is the eating behavior itself disrupting your day-to-day life? Is food missing? Are bathrooms messy? Is she eating your food? Or are you concerned with how the person is treating you? Perhaps meals are missed—she prefers eating alone to spending time with you; her emotional withdrawal has made you worry about the state of your relationship.

A goal in talking may be to bring up these matters as a means of working out food arrangements in the household or to help rectify difficulties you're now having in your relationship together.

For example, one woman wanted to bring up the issue of her roommate's bulimia in order to change the household food arrangements. Because her roommate always ate all the food, she wanted to shop separately and have separate food shelves.

In another situation, a mother and father wanted to speak with their compulsively overeating daughter about spending time with the family. One goal they had was to work out a way in which their daughter could join them for family occasions without there having to be pressure about eating.

Chapters 7, 8, and 9 will help you plan for, evaluate, and carry through the specific changes that need to be made in your situation. Be sure to read these chapters before instituting any new plans.

What is important now is to make clear why you are having this discussion and what you would like to see happen. Do not expect that the goals will be accomplished now. For example, if you need to discuss how food is handled in the house, don't try to work it out now. Set up another time to do this. Everything does not have to be worked out in one discussion.

HELPING HER GET THE HELP SHE NEEDS. An important goal may be in helping her acknowledge and accept she has an eating problem. She may already know this, and may even have contacted professionals. Or this may be the first time she is talking about it with someone. If encouraging her to seek help is your goal, tell her you're concerned about her health and welfare and that it is terrible to suffer alone with a problem. Offer your help in finding a suitable person to speak with, a support group to attend, or a physician for a physical evaluation. (Chapter 6 will discuss at length the resources available to both you and the sufferer.)

5. ***You can practice the discussion with someone.*** If there is a family member or friend who is aware of the eating problem, you can practice what you'd like to say before you actually speak with the eating-disordered person herself. Tell that person what it is you want to say. Ask him or her to respond by saying the type of things you are worried your daughter, spouse, or friend will say. This way, you'll have had time to anticipate some of the difficult spots and when the real situation occurs, you'll be more prepared to handle it. If there is no one else who is aware of the problem, respect the privacy of the person you care about. A support group is a good place to practice what you would like to say. In these groups, con-

fidentiality and the anonymity of the eating-disordered person can be maintained. (See Chapter 6 for more information on support groups.)

6. ***You can stop the conversation before it gets out of control.*** Keep this in mind when thinking about what you will say. This discussion is most likely going to be difficult and, if you are not careful, can lead into a battle of wills. Remember, it will be up to *you* to keep the conversation from becoming a fight, no matter what the reaction of the other person is. Let your concern show. If you find, though, in the discussion that you become angry or upset, STOP THE CONVERSATION before it gets heated and hurtful. You should tell the person that you want to continue talking at a time when you are not so upset. Tell her you'd like to try again, maybe under different circumstances or with someone else present.

It is not necessary that everything be said at once. You will have made a start. Continuing when emotions are heated will only make things worse. It is okay to try again at another time.

7. ***If you are worried that the situation is an emergency you will need professional guidance as to how to proceed.*** Tell the person that you are going to call a professional for advice as to what to do next. Read Chapter 5, "Emergency Situations," for more information as to what to do now.

ANTICIPATING REACTIONS

You cannot easily predict how someone is going to respond to your overtures. A variety of reactions is possible and your response will vary depending on what happens. The following sections detail some of the reactions that people commonly have when they are approached about an eating problem.

Relief

For some people, knowing that someone else is aware of the problem affords great relief. They're not alone anymore with their secret and now there's someone to help them.

Joann, a 20-year-old bulimic, referred to her discussion with her mother this way:

> After my mother told me that she knew I was bulimic and that she wanted to help me, I felt calm for the first time in a year. I could stop pretending everything was all right with me. I could talk to my parents about some of my feelings. I had been so worried that if my mother found out, she wouldn't be able to take it. Now I didn't have to think about that anymore.

Expressed relief may actually come much later, even years after the confrontation. Marianne, 18, looks back to when she was 15 and her parents insisted she see a psychiatrist for anorexia:

> I remember screaming at the top of my lungs—no way was I going to some shrink. I was terrified my parents would make me gain weight. I hated them and I told them so. They didn't know what was best for me.
>
> Only now can I admit that I also remember this other feeling underneath saying, "You can stop now. You don't have to fight anymore. You're going to be able to eat." Everything felt quiet inside for the first time in a long time, like a life preserver had been thrown out to me. I remember I just started to cry.

Admission of a Problem

Sometimes once someone realizes other people are aware of the problem, the person herself is able to admit something is really wrong.

Shelly, a 19-year-old college junior, binged and vomited every night after classes. Because she and her roommate Derrie lived in such close quarters, she was sure Derrie knew. Even though Shelly never ate or threw up in front of her roommate, Shelly knew Derrie saw the food and smelled the bathroom odors.

> Derrie was pretty thin herself so I just figured she thought the bulimia was not such a bad thing—like I had a good trick to lose weight. But one night Derrie told me that she knew I was bulimic and that she was really upset about it. She said she thought I needed help. I was shocked. I had thought all along that she didn't think it was so bad. When she said this to me, I was embarrassed and for the first time really worried. It was like I finally had to look at what I was doing. Up until then I thought maybe it wasn't so bad if Derrie didn't think so. It was only after that night that I realized I was in trouble and should go for help.

Some of you may have the fortunate experience of broaching the subject and finding that the person you are worried about is not only aware of the problem but is already in treatment. An important goal has already been achieved and the road has been paved for an open discussion. (Move on to Chapters 7, 8, and 9.)

Defense and Denial

Not everyone confronted about an eating disorder will react like the women just described. You may find that the person you're approaching denies that a problem exists. Anorexics in particular often do not feel they have a problem, and they'll do everything they can to convince you they don't. Bulimics and compulsive overeaters at first may feel nothing but the shame of being found out. Relief is the last thing on their minds at that moment. Remember, you may be the first person talking to them about a secret they have harbored for years. Your concern may be met with any one of a variety of angry responses.

"HOW DARE YOU!"

The person may get furious at you. She may feel intruded upon, embarrassed, found out, and she will react defensively to keep you away. She'll tell you there is no problem—she doesn't know what you are talking about. Be prepared for this possibility—no one likes being confronted with a secret she is ashamed of. It's important for you to remember that anger is a normal response to the subject you're bringing up. The anger is masking shame and fear, and at this stage of the game, the person may think you are trying to take something away from her.

Be prepared. If you anticipate an angry scene in advance, you'll be better equipped to react to it without getting upset yourself. Don't be intimidated by what the person says. No matter what she is saying, she may very well need you at this point. (Remember Marianne who only years later could admit her relief at being found out.) Hold your position and repeat why you are concerned. Remember, no matter what the person says, this is not a time for *you* to react angrily too. It's likely you'll feel angry but this is not the time to express it.

"MIND YOUR OWN BUSINESS"

The person may tell you it's not your business. It's her life and she can do what she wants. She'll tell you you're always butting in and that if you stopped worrying about her, maybe she wouldn't have a problem in the first place. She'll tell you she can handle things herself. In this case, tell her how her problem *is* affecting you, how she's made it your business. If you are someone close to her, you might tell her what she has done to make you worry, like losing a frightening amount of weight, isolating herself, or bingeing). Tell her she can't expect someone who cares about her to ignore these behaviors. If you live with her, perhaps she's regularly eaten all the household food or spent long hours in the bathroom when you want to use it. That is certainly your business. Tell her that if she could handle things herself, she wouldn't have given you cause to worry. That's why you feel you have to intervene.

Regardless of exactly what you say, remain firm. Remember, too, that all of this will be useless if it is said in an angry, accusatory tone. You can be insistent without being upset or demanding.

"YOU'RE NOT SO GREAT YOURSELF"

Since the best defense is a good offense, you may find yourself attacked when you bring up this issue. The person may tell you that you're no judge of how someone should eat because you're too fat yourself. Or she might say that *you* diet all the time—what gives you the right to say anything? You count calories too. You worry about your weight. Or she may accuse you of other problems—your drinking, your poor relationships, your own vices and/or fears. She'll know exactly what to say to make you question yourself.

Don't get pulled into these discussions. It doesn't matter what your problems are at this moment. In fact, you might tell her that if she is worried about something you do, you two can find another time to talk about it. That is not the issue right now. You might start to feel insecure about what you're saying—"How *can* I help? I have my own problems." If you start to say this to yourself, STOP! Of course you have problems—we all do—but this doesn't mean you can't be helpful to someone else.

"YOU'RE WRONG"

The other person may simply say that you're wrong. She'll tell you that you're just panicking or that you're not living with her, so how could you know anyway? She'll tell you everyone diets and that she's no different—or that she has a nervous stomach and the vomiting has nothing to do with bulimia.

You must remember that it is always possible that you *are*

wrong. Because you suspect a problem does not always mean that one exists. Tell the other person that you realize this is a possibility. You are prepared to be wrong. However, point out what you *have* seen, why you *are* worried. Tell her at this point that you still have questions and would like to talk about them.

NOW WHAT?

When Things Go Well

The other person may be able to acknowledge that she too is concerned about herself. Or she may disagree that a problem exists but seems willing to talk. She may start out resentful but is ultimately able to consider what you have to say. In these cases, you have gotten off to a good start.

With the problem out in the open, it is now important that you follow through with the goals of your discussion. If you just wanted to let the person know you're concerned, then you have already accomplished what you set out to do. Perhaps you can discuss together how you may continue to be of support. Maybe you want to encourage the person to seek outside help. In fact, if it's a child or young teenager in question, you may need to arrange for the person's treatment yourself. If that is the case, Chapter 6, "Seeking Help," will guide you in the steps you need to take next. Perhaps you want to speak with the person about how her eating behaviors are interfering in your life or how you are concerned in general about your relationship with her. Chapters 7, 8, and 9 will provide guidelines for this.

Karen, a 16-year-old anorexic, describes her experience of being approached by her parents:

> I was eating less and less, but I felt so fat that no matter what my parents said about how thin I was, I still wouldn't eat. I could hear my parents arguing about what to do. My mother

wanted to leave me alone; she thought it was just a phase I was going through. My father was frightened and thought I should be forced to eat. That fight went on for a long time, and meanwhile I wasn't eating. Then one day, and I don't know how it happened, my parents together said they had to speak to me. I said I had nothing to say to them, but they said, "You don't have to say anything. Just listen."

Then they said, "We love you too much to let you do this to yourself. You're wasting away. You don't go out anymore, you don't see your friends, and we're worried. We spoke to a therapist who specializes in anorexia and we made an appointment for all of us to see her." At first I told them I wouldn't go. But neither one of them would budge. They said I had no choice. Usually when they would try to tell me what to do, I would get them off my back by listing all their faults. Sometimes I would just complain about one to the other. I tried all this, but neither one took the bait—so here I am.

Deborah, a 26-year-old bulimic, was first confronted about her behavior by her husband:

I'd been married two years and I was bulimic the whole time. Before I was married, I'd been bulimic for eight years. For two of those years I was still living with my family. I ate more food at dinner than anyone in the family combined, yet I was the thinnest.

After meals I would spend an hour throwing up in the bathroom. No one ever said anything.

Then I got married and did the same thing, and my husband never said anything either. So I figured if they didn't care about me, why should I? I really thought no one noticed. But one day, my husband said he had to talk to me. He told me how hard it was for him to bring this up. He was afraid I would be angry at him, but he said he couldn't live with himself any longer if he didn't say anything. He said my health was more important than my being angry at him. He knew I was bulimic

> and he said he was scared about what that meant for him and for me. We were planning to have children and he was afraid it might interfere with my getting pregnant. It made him feel badly that I kept things secret from him. He wanted me to get some help—maybe go to therapy or attend a support group—and he said he would come too if that would help. He told me he loves me and would do anything to help me. He was crying when he told me all this and my husband never cried. Being bulimic makes me feel so ashamed that I never thought anyone would want me if they found out about it. His support made me able to face it myself.

Missed Attempts

Bringing up your concerns will not always go well. A mother called us in tears about a confrontation she'd had with her 17-year-old bulimic daughter, Kathy. She suspected her daughter was bulimic and had tried to speak to her about it:

> I knew something was wrong with Kathy. Food was disappearing from the kitchen and she never ate in front of anyone. I found empty laxative boxes in the wastebasket, and she spent much longer than anyone needs to in the bathroom. This morning I went to the bathroom. It stank from vomit. Something inside me snapped. I went into Kathy's room and screamed, "What's the matter with you? Are you sick? What kind of person does this kind of thing?" She was quiet and didn't say anything. I felt desperate to say something that would have an effect on her. The only thing I could think of to make her stop was this: I told her if she kept doing this, I'd tell all her friends. They thought she was Miss Perfect; wait until they heard this. She just looked at me like she could see through me and said, "Get out of my room, I hate you, I have nothing to say to you." I left the room, but now I don't know what to do next.

This mother, out of her frustration, approached her daughter in a way that led to misunderstandings, hurt, and anger. As many of us do in difficult situations, she had let the problem go on without saying anything, hoping it would go away, until she felt overwhelmed. She approached her daughter when she (the mother) was angry and, as a result, her daughter defended herself with angry silence and insults.

The mother's goal of stopping the bulimia was an impossible one—defeat was inevitable. It would have been less burdensome had she not walked in with such an overwhelming task on her hands. A more manageable goal would have been just to talk.

She also would have had a much better chance at being understood had she approached her daughter at a calmer moment. She and her daughter had a history of arguing. It may have been unrealistic to think she could have approached such a difficult issue without it ending once again in a fight. In this case, the mother needed support in handling her daughter. One way to achieve this would have been to speak with her husband before she said anything. If she felt she couldn't talk without getting upset, perhaps her husband could have approached their daughter or they may have done it together. If she were calmer she might have been able to speak to her daughter in a more collaborative manner. For example: "Kathy, we know you're having problems with food. We're concerned about how much you're eating; we've also heard you throwing up and that worries us. We want to help you with this and we want you to know we're here for you. Let's talk about what's going on."

In this case, the husband's presence might have tempered the reaction. If he were not available and the mother still worried about fighting with Kathy, it may have been helpful for the mother to talk first with a professional before speaking to her daughter. There was no reason that she *had* to do it alone.

In another situation, Marie called us about her husband George, whom she feared had a problem with food:

> George has always been overweight, but that's not really the problem. I don't mind big men. It's just that in the last few

> years all he seems to think about is food and his weight. He goes from one diet to another but nothing seems to work: within a week or two, he's eating whatever he wants again.
>
> The problem is that he never seems happy except for that first day or two he's on a diet. Then he feels hopeful and excited. But as soon as he "blows it," he's back obsessing about what he's eating and how heavy he is; he doesn't want to go out; he just mopes around the apartment—eating! Last weekend, I finally had it. We had been planning to go skiing and at the last minute (after blowing another diet, of course) he said he was too tired to go. I couldn't believe he was doing this again. I lost it. "You're not too tired," I yelled. "You're too fat—you don't have the energy to do anything except eat." He stopped speaking to me and I don't know what to do.

Marie, like Kathy's mother, approached her husband when she had lost control of her feelings. She was frustrated and disappointed and certainly was not in a position to be supportive. Because she was approaching George when he had let her down, it was unclear whether Marie's goal was to do anything but retaliate for the disappointment she had experienced. If Marie wanted to fight with George, that was one thing. But if she hoped to change the situation, she would need to speak to George when she had thought through what she'd like to say.

A more constructive way to approach George would have been for Marie to say: "George, I love you, but I'm worried about how you're eating all the time and how depressed you seem to be. I'm afraid for your health if you keep eating like this. We used to do things together like go skiing, and I miss that. Our relationship is suffering."

What to Do If It Doesn't Work

Bringing a problem out into the open is not always going to go smoothly. You may need to try more than once before you are able to express yourself in a way that can be heard and accepted. If so, let some time pass after your first encounter. Then broach the subject again.

In some cases, no matter what you do or say, there may be a steadfast refusal to talk or to acknowledge your concerns. When that happens, you have to decide what to do next. What you can do is the subject matter of the following chapter.

5

WHEN SHE SAYS NOTHING IS WRONG

Coping with Denial

What if the person you care about refuses to consider that a problem exists? She or he either denies a problem, insists nothing is wrong, or refuses to take the problem seriously.

Whether you merely suspect a problem or know that one exists, this is inevitably a difficult situation and you are going to need help. You cannot assess the seriousness of the situation or know what to do next on your own. The assessment of an eating disorder is a complex and difficult task. Even professionals cannot always tell if a problem is part of a temporary phase or whether it signals the beginning of a full-blown eating disorder. This is certainly not something that you should expect yourself to know.

YOU DON'T NEED TO GO IT ALONE

The best way for you to proceed is to contact a professional for a consultation. The purpose of a consultation in this situation is not necessarily for seeking treatment, but for receiving help in deciphering the seriousness of what you are observing, and, given the complexities of your particular situation, knowing what you can do. Consultations can be anywhere from one to a few sessions.

When you go for a consultation, you should let your daughter, spouse, or friend know that you take the situation seriously enough to speak with someone. You should let her know what you are doing, but it is not necessary for you to have her consent. Seeking help is for *you* to find a way of better coping with or handling a situation that is difficult for you.

There are many types of professionals or groups you can contact to help you know how to proceed. For example, you may want to contact an eating disorder specialist or center, a peer support group, or perhaps a hotline. If you are in a college setting, the available resources would include the college health services or a dorm counselor. In work settings, there may be Employee Assistance programs where counselors are available. The types of resources available are explained in Chapter 6. Consult the Resources section at the back of the book for organizations that will help you find therapists and treatment facilities in your community.

Before you actually call or set up an appointment to speak with someone, it is a good idea to organize your thoughts:

- Have a clear idea of the behaviors you see that are worrisome. Look over the checklists in Chapter 1 and make a list of the various signs and symptoms you've seen.
- Think about whether there has been a worrisome change in the person's behavior or mood. Can you tell when these changes began? How long have they been going on?
- If you know of or suspect any drug or alcohol abuse, let the consultant know of this.
- The consultant should be particularly alerted to any alarming behaviors such as talk of suicide, suicidal gestures, self-mutilating behaviors (for example, arm slashing). Does the sufferer complain of physical problems such as fainting, heart palpitations, or shortness of breath?

- Evaluate if and how the impact of the eating behavior has been disruptive in the household. For example, is food missing? Are bathrooms left messy? Are mealtimes stressful?
- If there has been a change in your relationship, let the consultant know what this change is and how long it has been going on. (For example, are you arguing more? Does she spend less time with you?)
- Tell the consultant what you have tried to do about the situation and what have been the results. Describe discussions or confrontations you have had with the person you're worried about, and what her reactions have been.

PLANS OF ACTION

Depending on your situation, some plans of action may work better than others. What you are advised to do will take into account how severe the situation appears to be, the person's age, her capacity to care for herself, and your relationship to her. What you are advised to do will also depend upon the leverage you have in the relationship, that is, the amount of control and/or influence you can exert in this particular relationship.

There are no clear-cut rules as to how to proceed. Each situation differs, and that is why the opinion of a professional or advice of a support group is necessary at these times. The following are some examples of how different families, spouses, and friends were advised to act in their particular situations.

The Steiner Family

This is what Mr. and Mrs. Steiner were advised to do with their 15-year-old visibly anorexic daughter who refused to acknowledge a problem or to see a therapist:

When Mrs. Steiner called us, her 15-year-old daughter Lee had already dropped from 110 pounds to 80 pounds. The Steiners had not called sooner because Lee had angrily refused to see anyone for help and they didn't feel there was anything they could do. But as Lee grew thinner and thinner and became isolated from friends, Mrs. Steiner felt they could no longer sit back.

We asked Mrs. Steiner how it was that an 80-pound little girl was more powerful than her parents. Lee was potentially dying and she was not in a position to know what was best for her. How was it that she was the one making all the decisions? We told Mrs. Steiner that she had to bring Lee in for a consultation. This was not to be Lee's choice.

Mrs. Steiner feared a scene. She imagined herself and her husband literally carrying a kicking, screaming teenager into our offices. We realized this was possible, but still a better option than letting Lee die. With our urgent support behind the Steiners, an interesting thing happened. Mr. and Mrs. Steiner were able to be forceful (verbally, not physically) with Lee and Lee came into treatment—sulking but without the tantrum we had all expected. What was clear was that in other attempts to get Lee in for a consultation, the Steiners had backed down when Lee got angry. When Lee realized her parents meant business, she yielded to their authority.

The Robertson Family

In another situation a parents' support group encouraged the parents of an anorexic daughter to use financial leverage as a way of bringing their daughter into treatment. There are times when withdrawal of financial support may be helpful as a means of showing that you mean business. A symptomatic daughter who is in a life-threatening situation cannot have the freedom to make her own decisions. The Robertsons are an example of how one family used the withdrawal of money to intervene in a potentially harmful situation.

Jenny and Lou Robertson attended a parents' group because they were desperate about how to handle the situation with their 26-year-old daughter Carey. Carey was planning to spend the year abroad, pursuing her career in art history by attending classes in Italy and France. Her acceptance to these classes was a long-awaited opportunity and the Robertsons had decided to pay Carey's expenses as a belated graduation gift. Carey had spent the previous year eagerly planning and anticipating this move. In the past three months, however, the Robertsons grew concerned that something was wrong. It seemed as if Carey had stopped eating.

Whenever the family got together, she refused meals, choosing to go to her room and exercise instead. She repeatedly asked her older sisters whether she looked fat. When Carey and her mother went shopping for clothes for the trip, Mrs. Robertson realized that her once-normal-weight daughter had dropped at least three clothing sizes in the last several months. In fact, they had to go to the children's department to find anything that would fit. Carey was delighted. Mrs. Robertson was horrified. She could see her daughter was not well—and was about to leave the country for a year!

The members of the support group insisted that the Robertsons question why they were going to support Carey's trip to Europe when Carey was clearly anorexic and in trouble. The Robertsons protested the group's suggestion. This was a promise they had made to their daughter. She had been planning this for a year. Wouldn't she get worse if they withdrew their support? Wouldn't she hate them for doing this?

The group remained firm. They told the Robertsons that they had to tell Carey that they could not pay for this trip because she was in trouble and needed help. She was not taking care of herself in the States; how would she feel alone in Europe? Carey had to see a professional in New York who could determine whether she was healthy enough to continue plans for the trip. It might be possible that help could be set up for her in Europe. Chances were more likely, however, that Carey would need to postpone the trip until her feet were on the ground.

The Robertsons ended up taking the group's advice, but dreaded the confrontation with Carey. When they spoke to Carey, they told her that they would be ignoring a serious problem if they supported the trip. They said that their financial support would be contingent upon her going for a consultation and having a professional determine whether she was healthy enough to go. Carey blew up. "You promised me," she screamed. "I can't believe you're backing out of a promise. I've been looking forward to this for a year and now you say something? If you're so worried, why didn't you say anything sooner?"

With the "voices" of the parents' support group behind them, the Robertsons held firm. "We're sorry we didn't take this action earlier," they said. "We have given this a lot of thought, and we're afraid that if we go along with the trip we'll just be failing in our responsibility to you. We feel horrible about this but we can't ignore how troubled you seem."

Carey screamed that she wasn't troubled—*they* were troubled and they were certainly going to make her troubled now. She told her parents they weren't trustworthy and that they were ruining her life. Carey's remarks stung, but they kept telling themselves that the group (and even they themselves) knew this was the right decision. Ultimately there was nothing Carey could do. Mrs. Robertson set up the consultation herself and both parents accompanied Carey to the meeting. The therapist agreed that Carey was in deep trouble and supported the Robertsons in postponing the financing of the trip.

Despite being upset, however, Carey started treatment.

Doing what the Robertsons did is not easy. Carey was enraged at their decision, insisting she was okay. However, if the Robertsons had backed down, they would have neglected a part of Carey that could only speak up through the weight loss—the skinny, scared little girl who felt overwhelmed by the prospect of a year in another country. By telling Carey they would not endorse or pay for the trip at this point, they were acknowledging Carey's inability to take adequate care of herself at that time.

Ben and Janet Walker

If you are married to someone with an eating disorder, you cannot make unilateral decisions about your spouse. Taking a firm stand about how the problem is hurting you, your spouse, and your relationship will usually get the person's attention and often her cooperation.

Benjamin Walker, 35, describes how he approached his wife Janet, 33, about her bulimia:

> For months, things seemed to be going wrong in our marriage. Janet complained I worked too much; I thought she was depressing to be around—always complaining about her weight when I thought she looked fine. I know the two of us were spending less and less time together—to be honest, I think I was hiding out in my work. But one weekday I got a call at work from our friend, Liz. Liz said that every time she called Jan, she was told that it was a "bad time." "Is she okay?" Liz wanted to know. "I haven't seen her in weeks and she and I used to speak every day."
>
> Liz's call jolted me. I knew Jan was bulimic and I wondered if that's what was wrong. After Liz's call, though, I started to pay more attention. I noticed that Janet was in the bathroom far too often, and when she wasn't in the bathroom, she'd be eating. It occurred to me that not only was Jan putting Liz off, but she wasn't in touch with anyone anymore.
>
> I told Janet I wanted to speak with her. We had talked about the bulimia before but not like this. I told her that I knew things weren't great between us and that I was worried that I was making her sick. I told her what I'd been observing and about Liz's call. I was trying to be caring and open, but

she just looked at me and said, "You're not making me do anything." I wanted to know what she was going through. She said, "Nothing. Why are you suddenly so interested anyway?" I couldn't believe she was being so cold when I was trying to reach out to her. That morning was a disaster. I started yelling at her and she cried; we ended in silence.

I guess, though, that it scared me. In the afternoon I found the name of a bulimia hotline and spoke to them about Jan. They suggested that I try again but in a different manner.

This time I stayed firm. I told Jan that our marriage was in trouble. We could either let it die or try to do something about it. I wanted to talk about what we could do. I told her that for the marriage to work, I needed her to speak to someone about her bulimia. But it wasn't all up to her; I wanted to know what she needed from me.

I think that this way of talking surprised Jan. I guess she expected more of an attack. When I told her that I was willing to do something too, she was more willing to talk to me. We went to see a family therapist. Once we were in treatment, Jan was able to talk about how her worries about our marriage made her want to block everything out by eating. She acknowledged her eating problem and began to work on it. On my part, I had to deal with my own eagerness to retreat through working.

In fact, the therapist kept saying that my working was as much of an addiction as Jan's eating. We both had a lot of work to do to get our marriage back on track.

Laura and Jessica—Roommates

In some cases, particularly when friends and colleagues are involved, you will not be advised to further confront the sufferer. Instead, a professional or counselor (such as a dorm counselor or Employee Assistance Program counselor or teacher) will intervene directly by speaking to the person herself. Laura and Jessica were in such a situation.

Laura and Jessica were roommates at a midwestern university. They didn't know each other before rooming together but by luck they got along perfectly.

When they first arrived at school and were homesick, they could talk to each other. No matter what happened at school or socially, whether times were exciting or disappointing, they could handle it together. Freshman year was turning out better than either had hoped.

Then in the second semester, Laura noticed a change in Jessica. Suddenly Jessica always had an excuse for why she wasn't coming to the dining hall. Before, they would order pizzas when they had a late study night. Now Jessica was never hungry. She didn't want late night snacks. Laura thought Jessica's behavior was strange and she asked Jessica why she didn't seem to eat much anymore. Jessica would answer that she did eat, it was just at different times, and because Laura didn't see her didn't mean she wasn't eating.

Laura wanted to believe Jessica. She knew Jessica was losing weight, but Laura didn't think too much about it. One night when Jessica thought Laura was sleeping, Jessica undressed in their room instead of in the bathroom. Laura was horrified. She'd never seen anyone in the flesh who looked so thin. The only people Laura had seen that looked like that were in photographs: they were the pictures of concentration camp survivors. But no one who had access to food could look like that.

Laura didn't know what to do. The dorm counselor had lectured all the residents about anorexia and its effects. She wanted to help Jessica but knew if she told the counselor, Jessica would never speak to her again. If she didn't tell anyone, Jessica might die. Then again, this could just be a phase and Jessica would start eating again. Perhaps Laura could figure out some way to help Jessica that wouldn't involve telling any of the school authorities.

Unfortunately, Jessica would hear nothing of Laura's concern. She told Laura to mind her own business. Laura was stunned. Jessica had never spoken to her like this before. "I can't stand to watch you do this to yourself," she told Jessica. "You need help. I'm going to speak to our dorm counselor."

"Speak to whoever you want," Jessica sarcastically responded.

Laura did speak to the counselor, who then insisted on speaking with Jessica. School authorities were alerted and Jessica's parents were contacted. Laura's actions resulted in Jessica's taking a year's leave from school, going into a treatment facility, and getting help.

"I hated Laura that whole year," says Jessica, now 22 and recovered from anorexia. "But now I think she saved my life."

NO TIME TO WASTE: EMERGENCY SITUATIONS

Some situations are emergencies and you will be advised to act immediately to ensure the well-being of the person you care about. In these cases, an immediate treatment evaluation is imperative. The situations we are referring to involve the potential of suicide, physical harm, or death due to starvation.

Suicide attempts are not uncommon among bulimics. The despair and torment associated with bulimia combined with the bulimic's wish to get rid of pain quickly and impulsively can result in the wish to die. If someone tries to kill herself, if she makes a gesture (such as toying with a razor blade on her wrist), if she even just *tells* you she wants to kill herself, there is reason to consider the situation an emergency. You need to call for help at once. In these cases, it is better to overreact than do nothing.

In some situations talk of suicide can be a daily occurrence in which you are held hostage. Although each threat may not require an intervention, you should not evaluate this on your own: professional surveillance is needed.

The other emergency situation involves the possibility of death due to physiological damage. While death occurs less often among bulimics than anorexics, there have been cases of heart failure in both populations. Anorexics can die of many complications secondary to starvation, in particular fluid and electrolyte imbalances. "Fluid imbalance" means that the person is dehydrated; "electrolyte imbalance" refers to potassium depletion, which can cause heart failure. Unfortunately, these imbalances often occur without overt signs of something being wrong. Therefore, it should be considered an emergency if someone faints, collapses, or is too weak to walk. While you may know that someone is severely eating disordered by her low weight or constant vomiting, the signs of physical deterioration we have just described may be the only way of knowing that the person might be courting death. Again, you must act immediately and call for help.

In these cases, you will likely be advised that the person is in serious danger and requires immediate attention. If you are a parent, spouse, or perhaps friend, this means that you will be told to take the person to a hospital or a doctor for evaluation at once. Don't expect the other person to be a participant in getting help. Certainly you want to approach her in the manner we have been describing all along. Be calm and firm. Tell the person why you are alarmed, why the situation must be taken seriously, and what you are going to do (i.e., that you will take her to a doctor or a hospital for an evaluation). Certainly hear her out; give her time to talk. But it's likely that this will not be a good time for a calm discussion. Anticipate that she may refuse to go; it is likely you will be met with a fight. But no matter how fierce her battle, she has no choice here. When someone is this physically debilitated or psychologically distressed, she is not in the position to be able to judge what is best for her. You must do *whatever* is needed to make sure she will receive immediate professional help.

If you are an acquaintance, roommate, or if you are not an adult yourself, you may not be in the position to assist the person on your own. If that is the case, other professionals (such as school or dorm counselors) may intervene to take care of the person in trouble. If there are no authorities or professionals available you may need to contact the family. This is not the time to worry about politeness or confidences; someone may be in real danger.

WHEN YOU NEED TO LEAVE IT BE

As contrasted with emergency situations, there are times when the best thing to do is to leave the situation alone. Eating disorders have received a lot of attention in the media of late and you may find yourself sensitized to and worried about eating behavior that is not a signal of a serious problem, but part of a phase. These are times when you will be advised that your worries are ill-founded. In this situation, it is best to leave things alone and not pursue the matter with the other person. In these cases, pushing the issue when you've been told to leave it alone might only create a power struggle in which the other person may continue eating (or not eating) as a way of doing what *she* wants to do, not what *you* want. A problem can develop where none would otherwise have existed.

ACCEPTING YOUR LIMITATIONS

No matter what action is called for, even in the most extreme circumstances, there will always be limits to how effective you can be in influencing someone else's behavior. You may not be able to ensure that someone seeks or stays in therapy or, even if she does, that anything will change.

Shelley and Sue (both 24) shared living space when they each moved to New York to pursue careers in acting. When Sue noticed that food was continually missing from the refrigerator, she realized her roommate was having an eating problem. Messy bathrooms and Shelley's low weight pointed to the likelihood that Shelley was bulimic.

> I spent many weeks trying to get Shelley to talk about it, but she wouldn't. The situation was bad—at times she would eat and vomit all day long. Meanwhile I was spending endless amounts of money replacing *my* food. We'd work out some agreement for her not to eat my stuff—and then she'd do it anyway. I tried to talk to her about getting help but that was hopeless. She said she could stop if she wanted to. Finally, I just decided that there was nothing else I could do. I packed up my belongings and moved out.

Shelley remained bulimic for years after Sue moved out. In another situation, an anorexic's parents had tried to insist on therapy by cutting off their daughter's finances. This daughter angrily sidestepped her parents' intervention by withdrawing money from her savings to pay for the classes her parents had stopped funding.

In such situations, you are going to have to face the difficult limits of being a parent, spouse, or friend. No matter what you do, the other person is not going to change her behavior or seek help until she is capable of accepting the seriousness of the matter herself. You are not going to be able to make her see what you see or do what you may know is best.

When you are faced with this type of situation, there is no need to sit alone with your feelings. Join a support group or seek other types of counseling yourself. The suggestions of others who are going through similar experiences and/or the guidance of a professional can help you better cope with the situation. In these settings, you can voice your fears, disappointments, and frustrations and you'll receive the support necessary to face the limitations involved in trying to help someone who is potentially in serious trouble.

No matter how severe the problem is or what type of relationship you have, you will need to find ways of dealing with the impact of the eating behavior on your life. Chapters 7, 8, and 9 are devoted to discussing the process of *your* recovery. Even when there is nothing you can do about someone else's life, there are many things you can do about changing the effect the eating disorder has on your life, and the relationship you have with the sufferer.

6

NO ONE CAN GO IT ALONE

Seeking Help

Eating disorders represent serious psychological problems. In most cases, the intervention of professionals can make a significant difference in facilitating recovery and can ease the burden that you may be feeling to help the person get well.

Therapists, support groups, hospitals, and medical professionals are available to both sufferers and their families. Whether it is to make an evaluation of the problem or to undertake the treatment process, professionals are there to provide help and a consultation can provide useful information.

In the first section of this chapter, we review treatment, both medical and psychological for the eating-disordered person. Later in the chapter, we will review the type of help that is available to *you*. No matter what situation you are facing, an informed attitude about treatment options can make the process of coping and recovery smoother for everyone.

TREATMENT PLANNING FOR THE EATING-DISORDERED PERSON

When someone who is eating disordered is in need of services she should be seen for a consultation with a professional who can help outline the type of treatment approach that would be most beneficial. The professional best qualified to make these treatment plans would be a therapist who is experienced in eating disorders.

A treatment plan will take into account many factors, including the duration and severity of the illness, the family situation, and other substance abuse. The consultant will consider the situation and will then recommend a course of treatment that may include work with different specialists or groups.

The various types of treatment that might be suggested for the eating-disordered person include psychotherapy, support groups, medical or psychopharmacological intervention, and nutritional counseling. In some cases hospitalization may be recommended.

Psychotherapy

In many cases, the most effective means of treating the eating-disordered patient is through the process of psychotherapy. The three types of psychotherapy are individual, family (including couples treatment), and group therapy. The type of therapy recommended will depend on the age, needs, and living situation of the person seeking treatment.

Another factor that is evaluated in treatment planning is whether the person has any other problems in addition to the eating disorder. Is she, for example, a multiple abuser who also has trouble with drugs and/or alcohol? Most professionals agree that alcohol and drug abuse need to be controlled *before* active work on the eating disorder is undertaken. Thus treatment planning will need to take this into account.

An assessment should also be made of other factors in the life and family of the eating-disordered person. Is there gambling, incest, alcohol, drug abuse, or violence at home? Sometimes treating someone with an eating disorder will involve addressing these issues in family or couples therapy. Therefore, a treatment plan needs to consider all these possibilities.

INDIVIDUAL PSYCHOTHERAPY

In individual psychotherapy, the patient meets with the therapist alone. Sessions are held a minimum of once a week, usually lasting 45 minutes per session.

Individual psychotherapy of the eating-disordered person should involve working with the visible symptoms of bingeing, purging, or starving and the more "invisible" psychological factors.

The eating behavior itself needs to be discussed. Indeed this is what is foremost on the person's mind. The person in therapy works to understand the role that eating or purging has served in her life, and finds replacements for the destructive behaviors while developing healthier coping mechanisms.

As she explores her inner world and her experiences with people, she comes to understand why and how eating (or starving) has become her means of coping. Why is it that food is safer than turning to people? Why does nothing feel as soothing as the eating or purging? What keeps getting in the way of her resolve to stop bingeing? What would be on her mind if she weren't worried about her weight?

Not every type of individual psychotherapy will address underlying feelings and thoughts. The treatment we endorse is one which will focus on changing the eating behaviors without losing sight of the reasons why food is used in the first place. The goal of treatment should not be merely to stop the behavior, but to understand *how* and *why* the person has used food to attempt to meet developmental and emotional needs. Don't assume that because someone is a therapist that he or she will necessarily work in this fashion.

There are two pitfalls that should be avoided. The first is where the symptom is focused on to the exclusion of its purpose in the person's life. If treatment addresses the visible aspects of the problem and does not consider what is unseen—the psychological factors—the problem is apt to continue via other means. Many women switch from food to alcohol or drugs in their attempts to control their eating. Without understanding the way the food helps them, they merely replace one addiction with another.

The other pitfall involves a treatment focus that is concerned *solely* with the inner world of the patient. We hear too often of therapy that has been going on for many years and food is not discussed *at all*. This is like treating an active alcoholic without addressing the alcohol abuse. When someone is actively bingeing or starving and it is not being discussed, only half the person is in the treatment room.

One of the main benefits of individual therapy is that it provides a one-to-one relationship with the therapist, in which the person in treatment can acknowledge and explore her feelings and thoughts. As the eating-disordered person is more fully able to accept herself as well as her feelings about others, the need to block out parts of herself through food can be lessened. One aspect of this is helping her differentiate feelings from physiological hunger. People with eating disorders tend to misinterpret internal emotional experiences as hunger and respond by eating.

The therapist should be a person who is not involved in the patient's personal life. He or she should not be a relative or friend of the family. This way, the patient can feel assured that the therapist has no personal investment in what she does and she can feel safer to reveal feelings and thoughts about herself, family, and/or friends.

FAMILY THERAPY

In family therapy, sessions involve not just the eating-disordered person but members of her family. This may include her parents and siblings, her spouse (if she is married), and possibly grandparents or other relatives who may be immediately involved or living with her.

In family therapy, the eating disorder is seen as a "red flag." It signals that troubles exist in the family as a whole, not just with the eating-disordered person. Difficulties in the family may include marital problems, lack of ability to communicate feelings, difficulty setting rules, difficulty in expressing conflict, or the inability to enjoy one another. These types of issues are explored openly with all family members; to solve the family's problems all members are encouraged to change, not just the member with the eating disorder.

Family therapy is essential when the symptomatic person is a child living at home. When the person is an adolescent, family therapy may be recommended in conjunction with individual therapy. The course of therapy, frequency of meetings, and the participants in the sessions will vary depending on the severity of the disorder and the specific family situation. Sometimes parents may be seen without their daughter, regardless of whether the daughter is or is not in individual therapy. If you are the spouse of an eating-disordered person, you may find that couples therapy, which is a form of family therapy, is recommended for you and your wife. Lastly, parents may be called in periodically to join their daughter in her individual sessions for what is called a "joint session." In all of these cases, the goal is still the same. Members work to explore and change patterns of interacting that interfere with each individual's growth and with the family's functioning.

GROUP THERAPY

A group usually consists of 5 to 12 people who meet with a therapist on a weekly basis. This treatment approach is particularly helpful in countering feelings of isolation or of being all alone with the problem. A group can provide feedback and support while someone is attempting to change eating patterns. It is also a safe place for members to learn new ways of relating, to express feelings, and to develop trusting relationships that can substitute for the self-destructive relationship to food.

There are different types of groups. Some focus specifically on the eating and its meaning and function in someone's life. In these groups, the members may concentrate on how and when the eating behavior occurs. Group members support one another in finding ways to change the eating patterns and develop healthier coping styles. Sometimes group members may call one another for support when they are having a rough time with the urge to binge. These types of groups are usually time-limited, organized to last anywhere from several weeks to several months.

Other groups are more insight-oriented and do not focus exclusively on the eating behaviors but address underlying emotional dilemmas as well. They are usually open-ended in duration.

The difference between the two types of situations is highlighted by Terry's experience:

Terry, 25, had been attending a behavior-oriented group in addition to her individual therapy. The group focused on learning what triggered the members' urges to binge and how to develop alternatives to the bingeing behavior. Terry was now looking to move on:

> As a result of this group and my individual therapy, I am able to control my bingeing most of the time, and because of this I rarely vomit. But now I need to take the next step. I want a group that is less focused on food and more on interaction. I know I've used food to avoid people. I need to see what scares me so much about relying on people.

Terry was referred to an insight-oriented group in which she was able to explore her relationships with group members as a way of understanding why she believed that food was more dependable than people.

Groups are not usually recommended for the treatment of acute anorexia. Anorexics who are severely restricting their food intake are not able to relate well enough to others to benefit from the interaction. Their cognitive and social capacities are so impaired from starvation that it is impossible for them to concentrate on relationships with other people. In addition, these young women are so intensely competitive to be the thinnest in the room that the usual good feelings that arise from the experience of shared problems and mutual support do not develop. Because of this, the development of trust and mutual respect does not occur.

Support or Self-Help Groups

Whether or not someone is in psychotherapy, support or self-help groups can be a valuable means of getting help with the problem and feeling less isolated. These groups consist of people at varying stages of recovery who meet to share experiences, suggestions, and camaraderie. For many people, self-help groups are a first step in realizing they are not alone and that change *is* possible.

Support and self-help groups can meet anywhere from daily to once a month. As the name implies, they are not psychotherapy groups and thus are not usually run by a therapist. A leader is present to structure the group meeting. Sometimes the leader is herself recovered from an eating disorder and can use her own experience as a source of inspiration and/or guidance for others. Because these groups do not employ the services of a trained professional, they are usually free or are run for a nominal fee to pay for the meeting space that is used. The groups can be attended as needed without participants having to make a commitment to join. As a result, membership can change from meeting to meeting.

Support groups vary in their structure. Some have no particular agenda, while in others a particular topic is discussed at each meeting. Some groups start with a speaker and then break into small discussion groups where participants explore their feelings about the subject discussed. Examples of topics that groups have picked to discuss include: "How eating disorders affect relationships," "What should you do if you're hungry?", "How to handle going home for Thanksgiving."

ANAD—National Association of Anorexia Nervosa and Associated Disorders has affiliated groups available nationally, and in Canada, West Germany, Austria, and Saudi Arabia. The working structure of ANAD groups include a rap group format, emphasizing shared feelings and personal growth through interaction and support. Discussion of food behaviors is discouraged in favor of discovering underlying problems and developing positive methods of coping with these problems. ANAD has developed an Eight-Step Program that provides structure and guidelines for support groups and individuals.

The principles are described in Meehan, Wilkes, and Howard (1984), *Applying New Attitudes and Directions* (see Suggested Readings).

A.A.B.A. (American Anorexia/Bulimia Association, Inc.) has affiliated support groups available in New York, Philadelphia, Virginia, and Florida. Included in these support groups are a professional and someone recovered from an eating disorder, and the groups work toward recovery.

Other organizations that help develop support groups are listed in the Resource section at the back of the book.

OVEREATERS ANONYMOUS

Overeaters Anonymous (O.A.) is a particular kind of self-help group based on the twelve-step program for recovery developed by Alcoholics Anonymous. Overeaters Anonymous is based on the philosophy that compulsive eaters are powerless over food and that eating disorders are lifelong addictions. Control over food is sought by helping one another resist the temptations of bingeing. O.A. now has meetings specifically for the bulimic and anorexic person.

O.A. has an extensive support network available for the person who may be craving food at all hours of the day. Members are encouraged to find a sponsor whom they can call when they need help abstaining from bingeing or purging. The sponsor is someone who is at a later stage of recovery and is available to people first entering the program.

Within the philosophy of O.A., abstinence is seen as the basis of recovery. However, for many eating-disordered people, abstinence is simply the opposite side of the coin from bingeing. They may be on the winning side of the battle but the war wages on. O.A. does not see the possibility of truly making peace with food. Yet while we believe, as do many others in the professional community, that eating disorders are curable, not merely controllable, for the majority of sufferers, there is a portion of the eating-disordered population that faces a chronic, lifelong struggle with food. For this group, O.A. offers a community that provides help in maintaining abstinence from bingeing which can be the best solution in the situation.

For others, the O.A. program can be turned to at different times during the process of recovery when support and structure are felt to be needed.

Medical and Nutritional Treatment

The varied physiological complications that result from disturbed eating behaviors require the attention of specialists, including internists, dentists, gynecologists, and nutritionists. During a treatment evaluation, the consultant may recommend that one or more of these professionals be seen to evaluate physiological damage or to provide specialized care in their area.

INTERNISTS

One cannot assume that an eating disorder is being comprehensively treated unless an internist is involved to assess the potential damages secondary to the eating disturbance. Unattended physical complications in all three disorders can lead to serious health problems and, in the worst case, death.

There are many destructive physical complications that can arise from problematic eating or purging patterns. For example, in anorexia common complications are lowered blood pressure, lowered body temperature, kidney and cardiac disorders, slow pulse rate, bloating, dry skin, and loss of menstrual cycle. When someone suffers from obesity due to compulsive overeating, heart, lung, and circulatory problems need to be evaluated. The symptoms of bulimia are varied. Some are troublesome, such as the loss of menstrual periods, decreased energy, light-headedness, and altered bowel habits. Others, such as irregular heartbeat, abdominal pain, muscle cramps, or loss of sensation may indicate serious complications. Dehydration and loss of important minerals are often the cause of these more serious disturbances.

When laxatives are used, which they might be in any of the three types of eating disorders, other complications can arise. Muscle and stomach cramps, chronic nausea, digestive problems, and physiological dependence are all possible effects of chronic laxative abuse.

If someone is seeing a therapist who specializes in eating disorders, the therapist will probably be able to recommend a physician. If not, you or the person in therapy may have to do some hunting around. It is important that professionals are chosen who are familiar with eating disorders and who take them seriously. If your child has shown a recent alarming weight drop and the physician says it is just a phase, look for another physician. If your wife is vomiting to control weight and the doctors prescribe diet pills or Valium, you must press her to find another doctor.

Bulimia and anorexia have become widespread only in recent years, and many physicians remain ignorant of the severity and deteriorating course of these problems. The rule of thumb is that if a physician you've contacted does not have a recognition of and respect for the psychological components of these disorders, he or she is not yet sufficiently informed. Move on and find another. The national organizations listed in the Appendix can help guide you in locating informed medical services in your location.

Because the signs and symptoms of an eating disorder are sometimes hidden, it is important that the person see someone who knows the current medical literature on these disorders and who will know to look for the ways the symptoms manifest themselves. The person seeking help should also be encouraged to be open and frank with her physician about her eating behaviors. One bulimic woman went to an internist because she was concerned about the enlarged glands in her throat. She was examined, X-rayed, and treated for Hodgkin's disease before she was able to muster the courage to admit that she was bulimic. Chronic swollen glands are a common side effect of bulimia. The internist was unfamiliar with this, and the woman, so embarrassed about the bulimia, was willing to be treated for cancer before she could consider revealing her problem.

If both the physician and patient are open about issues such as bingeing, vomiting, laxative abuse, and starvation, the whole examination procedure will be much more productive.

DENTISTS

Someone who is vomiting frequently is susceptible to tooth decay as a result of enamel erosion from regurgitated stomach acids. Dentists can be the first to notice these signs of bulimia. A checkup by a dentist is important for anyone who is vomiting.

A well-informed dentist and an open discussion about the problem will facilitate the treatment. Dentists who are unaware that the tooth erosion is due to vomiting may repair the damage without suspecting that the problem is ongoing and damage to the teeth will continue. As one patient told us in a group:

> I was on my third set of caps and $10,000 poorer, and my dentist couldn't figure it out. Finally, after working on it in therapy, I got up the nerve to tell him what I was doing. He suggested a temporary solution of brushing my teeth with baking soda after I threw up. He told me that the base in baking soda helped counteract the acids from vomiting and that this would slow down the erosion until I was able to stop purging. He also knew to stop replacing my caps.

GYNECOLOGISTS

Complications due to anorexia and bulimia may also warrant the services of a gynecologist.

For example, endocrinological changes caused by weight fluctuations and poor nutrition can alter the menstrual and reproductive cycle. Irregular menstrual cycles or a cessation of menses results. Often a gynecologist is needed to monitor these irregularities. Bulimics or anorexics who are vomiting may want to know whether birth control pills will be effective if they are vomiting or taking high doses of laxatives. (In fact, a gynecologist prescribing birth control pills *must* be told of purging behaviors so that the effectiveness of this type of contraception can be assessed.)

If pregnancy is desired, the effects of vomiting, starving, and using laxatives must be taken into account. Someone whose menstrual cycle is irregular may have trouble getting pregnant. For the anorexic whose menstrual cycle has stopped, pregnancy is unlikely.

However, many bulimics do achieve conception. When conception is possible, the question then is, will the child be healthy? There is much to be learned about the effects and risks of chronic vomiting, starving, and laxative abuse on fetal development and health of the baby. Eating disorders sometimes result in malnutrition and evidence indicates that severe malnutrition during pregnancy can cause a permanent reduction in brain growth and development, with possible reduction in the baby's intellectual functioning.[1] If the person you know is pregnant or thinking about becoming pregnant, speak with her about this. Her gynecologist must be made aware of her disturbed eating patterns. Urge the person you know to speak with her doctor. She will probably be considered a high risk and can be monitored for the various endocrinological changes caused by the eating disorder.

Some women with eating disorders revert to more normal eating habits during their pregnancy. Gerry, 32, a daily binge-vomiter, told us:

> When I was pregnant and in a sense taking care of someone else, I was able to eat normally and I kept the food down. But after the baby was born, I went back to my old ways.

A gynecologist aware of current research in the area of eating disorders should be able to answer questions regarding conception, pregnancy, and fetal risk that concern the eating-disordered woman and her partner.

1. Sir Dugald Baird, *Journal of Biosocial Science*, VI, 113, (1974). R.W. Smithells et al., "Maternal nutrition in early pregnancy," *British Journal of Nutrition* 38, 3 (1977): 497–506; and *Nutrition and Fetal Development*, ed. M. Winick (John Wiley & Sons, 1974). H.A. Kaminetzky and H. Baker, "Micronutrients in pregnancy," *Clinical Obstetrics and Gynecology* 20, 2 (1977): 363–380; and R.M. Pitkin, "Nutritional support in obstetrics and gynecology," *Clinical Obstetrics and Gynecology* 19, 3, (1976): 489–513.

NUTRITIONAL COUNSELING

Some people with eating disorders have extremely chaotic eating patterns or have not eaten a "meal" in years. Nutritionists, who are trained to assess nutritional imbalances and develop dietary programs, can help recovering clients correct nutritional deficits and develop healthy eating habits, perhaps for the first time.

The work of a nutritionist can best be utilized when binge, purge, or starving behaviors have decreased, food is no longer used as a coping mechanism, and the person is choosing to eat due to physiological, not psychological hungers. In many cases, at that point, the eating-disordered person is able to resume a more healthy eating regime on her own. When she has trouble with this, nutritional guidance can be helpful. This guidance is most effective when it is one aspect of a broad treatment program.

Sometimes a nutritionist is sought to provide a diet as an *answer* to the problems with food. However, a diet is not the answer to an eating disorder. Many eating-disordered people are experts themselves on diets and food intake. They *know* what is healthy. They know the caloric intake of every morsel they put in their mouths. Some are professionals in the area of nutrition. This underscores that eating disturbances are not due to lack of information about a good diet, but have to do with psychological factors that keep people from putting this information to use. It is thus essential that the psychological aspect of the bingeing and its role in someone's life is worked with first. After this, the work with a responsible nutritionist can best be utilized.

Medication

A consultant may recommend medication. When this is the case, a psychiatrist familiar with the current research in eating disorders can meet with the sufferer to specifically evaluate psychopharmacological treatment. The psychiatrist who specializes in eating disorders is the best informed about the overall symptom picture. Many psychotherapists who specialize in eating disorders can recommend a psychiatrist familiar with eating disorders.

There is much experimentation currently being done regarding the effectiveness of medication on the suppression of eating-disordered behaviors. The most promising results have been with the use of antidepressants among a subgroup of bulimics. The focus of research is understanding what combination of medication and psychotherapy is optimal (including which antidepressant and at what dosage) to reduce bingeing and purging behaviors among bulimics. There is less evidence of antidepressants helping anorexics, who do not binge and purge, or compulsive overeaters.

Antidepressants are also used whenever there are signs of severe depression, extreme lethargy, loss of interest in life, and/or suicidal thoughts.

All antidepressants have side effects. These vary among the different medications. Some of these side effects, such as increased appetite, can be particularly difficult for the eating-disordered patient to manage. The benefits of medication need to be weighed against the side effects they engender.

Medication is not a substitute for developing internal capacities to cope with life and its stressors. Psychotherapy is a part of any effective treatment plan and is necessary to deal with the psychological aspects of the eating disorder.

We strongly advise against the use of any appetite suppressants for bulimics or compulsive overeaters. These are not to be confused with medication, no matter how they are presented; they should be avoided.

For many people, medication is unnecessary or not worth the side effects. Symptoms can be effectively treated through the use of therapy, group, or other support networks. For others, medication can be very helpful. There are rarely clear-cut answers as to who will be helped by medication. The purpose of a meeting with a psychiatrist is for him or her to use expertise and experience to make this determination. It is crucial to remember that medication is never enough by itself. Don't expect it to passively cure an eating disorder, or you and the sufferer will be sorely disappointed. There are no easy cures or simple answers. If medication is prescribed, it is most effective in conjunction with a well thought-out treatment plan including individual, group, or family therapy.

Hospitalization

When someone is in a psychologically self-destructive or a physically life-endangering condition, hospitalization may be necessary. (See "Emergency Situations" in Chapter 5.) This is often the case when someone who, at a severely low weight, faints or collapses. If there is the potential for suicide, or her daily functioning is severely impaired, then custodial care and/or intensive treatment is necessary. Impairment in functioning may mean that the person cannot concentrate for sustained periods, her emotions feel overwhelming, and/or the bingeing, purging, or starving behaviors are extreme. When someone is in this condition, outpatient treatment is not effective. The person needs more support and structure than is possible a few hours a week in therapy or support groups. In these cases, reducing the environmental stressors while providing structure and psychotherapy can be useful.

While hospitalization is essential in severe conditions, it is not always necessary to wait for such a crisis before it can be helpful. It need not be a last resort. When used thoughtfully and effectively, there are times that hospitalization can provide a safe environment in which the patient can regain the inner resources and experience the sense of control needed to cope in her daily life. It can provide an opportunity to interrupt the symptomatic eating patterns, and allow the person to explore areas of concern that could not be approached if the eating were out of control.

The initial evaluation process must weigh the extent to which symptoms interfere with the person's daily life and the potential benefit of in-patient care and compare this with the disruption hospitalization might cause. If hospitalization is recommended for extended treatment, it should be on a unit where there is a familiarity with eating disorders. A general psychiatric unit is not the answer.

A medical unit that attends solely to weight is also inadequate. There are now hospitals that have units that specialize in treating eating disorders. Choose one that includes intensive psychotherapy. The organizations listed in the Resources section can help you locate such facilities in your area.

Avoid facilities that are considered weight-loss centers or spas. These programs are not as interested in the emotional well-being of their clients as they are in weight loss. They are not the place for someone who is physically ill, nor are they the answer for treatment of severe eating disorders.

Hospitalization is a serious interruption to one's life. It can involve anywhere from several weeks to many months and should not be done lightly. If someone must be hospitalized, it should be in a unit that provides both psychological and physiological services, and should be pursued only after competent professionals agree that the benefits of hospitalization outweigh its disruptive aspects.

FINDING THE SERVICES THAT ARE NEEDED

There may be times when you are in the position of helping the person you care about find the professional services that she needs.

The ideal way to find good professional help is through personal recommendation. If you're looking for a psychotherapist, for example, you might ask your doctor, a school counselor, or teacher whom he or she would send a daughter to if she had this problem. Friends and relatives may also be good sources of information.

Perhaps you know people who are in or have been in treatment (even for problems other than eating disorders). Ask if they are satisfied and would recommend the person they are seeing. This therapist may not be experienced with eating disorders or may not want to work with a friend or acquaintance of a client, but he or she will likely be able to recommend a therapist who can help with eating disorders.

You might also seek out facilities (such as teaching hospitals or outpatient psychotherapy centers) in your area that specialize in the treatment of eating disorders. They will have the names of therapists and other medical specialists. You will find such facilities listed in the Yellow Pages or in local newspapers that have community services advertising sections. The American Psychiatric Association, American Psychological Association, National Association of Social Workers, and American Association of Marriage and Family Therapists have local chapters listed in the telephone directories under the name of your state or county.

The Resources section, page 213, in this book lists the names of organizations that maintain a professional referral network both nationally and internationally. They will be able to help you locate specialists and eating-disorder treatment facilities in your geographic location.

ANAD—National Association of Anorexia Nervosa and Associated Disorders has been extremely effective in establishing support groups throughout the world. If you are looking for a support group (or are interested in starting one), your best bet would be to call them directly. Information packets are available upon request to assist people in learning about the illness—what it is and what to consider in looking for a therapist. The packets provide a list of books and magazine articles, lists of available support groups or therapists, and personal responses to individual questions or concerns. These packets assist not only families and friends of the eating disordered, but students, school counselors, teachers, and health professionals as well.

Choosing a Therapist

If you are helping someone look for a therapist or choosing one for yourself or family, the process of a consultation is the best one we know of to evaluate a particular therapist. There are certain questions that are useful for people entering therapy to ask at the outset. As a parent arranging therapy for a minor, you may be in the position of asking these questions yourself, either on the phone or during a consultation with the therapist.

Questions for All Therapists

1. ***Ask about credentials.*** Choose a qualified practitioner who is licensed (or training toward licensure) in his or her respective discipline. Most therapists are trained as psychologists, psychiatrists or social workers. Licensing and credential requirements vary from state to state. Be sure the person you're meeting with is either in the process of being licensed or is already licensed. This in and of itself does not guarantee good training and high ethics, but it is a start.

2. ***Ask about the therapist's experience and views about treatment.*** A specialization in the area of eating disorders is helpful. If the person or family entering therapy has addictions other than food (i.e., alcoholism or drug abuse), you will want to make sure that the professional is knowledgeable about and experienced in the area of addictions, is informed about and supportive of Alcoholics Anonymous or similar support networks, and is capable of dealing directly with these other addictions in addition to the eating disorder.

You want to be sure the therapist has a compassionate view of the symptom, that he or she knows the eating behavior is related to attempts at coping with inner emotional difficulties such as problems of identity, conflicts, and maturation. You want to stay clear of people who view eating disorders as a lack of willpower or bad eating habits.

3. ***Find out how much treatment will cost.*** You will find a vast range in fees depending upon the type of services being sought. Most likely fees will be higher for private practitioners than for clinic facilities.

4. ***Inquire as to billing procedures.*** Is payment required each session or once a month?

5. ***Find out the policy on missed sessions.*** Many therapists charge for missed sessions. Can these appointments be rescheduled? Is the patient charged for vacations? In particular, if you are a parent paying for your child's individual or group therapy, will you be informed if she misses sessions? Parents and therapists have different preferences in this regard. Be sure you understand the policy before your daughter begins therapy so there won't be misunderstandings later on.

6. ***Find out about insurance reimbursement.*** If the person in treatment has insurance, she may be partially reimbursed for outpatient treatment costs if the policy covers "outpatient psychiatric services." If the insurance provides this type of coverage, check if there are requirements for reimbursement. The person may need to see someone who is licensed in order to receive reimbursement. Licensing involves passing a state licensing exam, practicing for a certain number of years, and maintaining good ethical standing in the professional community. Check whether the therapist meets these requirements. Also, be aware that not all professionals take insurance reimbursement as direct payment for services.

7. ***Find out the policy on family members calling the therapist.*** Some parents want to know how the therapy is going or how much longer it is going to take. Therapists have different positions regarding phone calls. Be sure from the outset that you know what the arrangement is, why it is set up that way, and (particularly if you are paying for therapy) whether it is one you can live with.

8. ***Discuss what will happen in a crisis.*** If you're arranging treatment for an adolescent, you might want to know how the therapist handles a crisis situation, such as if the teenager takes drugs or gets pregnant.

There are some situations in which you *should* be contacted by the therapist. For example, if the client is suicidal, and a minor, parents should be alerted; in the case of a married client, the husband should be called. There are some situations, however, that are more ambiguous. What if your 12-year-old daughter is taking drugs? What if an adolescent is pregnant? If you are the parents of a minor, you have a right to be contacted in certain types of situations in which your child may be in trouble. If you are a parent of someone older, or a husband or friend, your rights are less clear (even if you are paying for the therapy). At the start of therapy, discuss with the therapist how crises are handled and in what type of situations (if any) you will be contacted.

There are other questions that may be useful depending upon the type of therapy pursued.

For Individual Therapists

1. Find out how the eating behavior itself is approached in treatment. Is the eating behavior a focus of therapy or does the therapist believe that if *other* issues are talked about, the eating behavior will change?

2. Is medication used? If so, when and why?

3. Will other therapies (such as group or family) be used in conjunction with the individual treatment?

For Family Therapists

1. How does the therapist view the eating disorder?

2. Does the therapist want to see the entire family? If so, who is included in that? Is it only those people living in the house, or, if there is a stepfamily, does the therapist want to see both the custodial and noncustodial families? Will this include stepparents? Will they want to see the extended family such as grandparents or important aunts and uncles? And what about young children?

3. How often will the family be seen? Once a week, every other week, or once a month?

For Group Therapists

1. How is the eating disorder approached in the group? Is the group a behavior- or insight-oriented group?

2. Does the group function as a support group in which members are encouraged to call one another outside the group?

3. What are the ages of the group members?

4. Does everyone in the group have an eating disorder? If so, is the group mixed with bulimics, compulsive overeaters, and anorexics, or are the members suffering from the same disorder?

Evaluating the Therapist

One question that is frequently asked of all types of therapists is whether it is beneficial to have a therapist who has been eating-disordered herself or himself. This is not necessary. What is most important is for the therapist to have the empathy to feel for and understand the patient's experience. Psychotherapists do not need to have experienced myriad emotional problems from anxiety to depression to phobias to be helpful in treating these disturbances. Indeed it would be impossible to have experienced everything that one treats. In this regard, psychotherapy is not unlike medicine. If you are a doctor, you don't need to have had cancer in order to treat it.

Because someone has been eating disordered does not guarantee that he or she will be more understanding of the patient's experience. Sometimes a therapist is still so close to his or her own personal struggle with food that the therapist insists on seeing the patient's difficulties as similar to his or her own when that might not be the case. In any therapeutic situation, it is important that the therapist be free to understand the patient's own unique personal experience and not color it by thinking it similar to what he or she has gone through.

Regardless of whether a therapist is or is not eating disordered, it is also unlikely that he or she will tell you. Therapists do not usually share intimate details of their own history. Such information can be a burden to the patient.

What you or the patient *should* be concerned with is the therapist's training in the area of eating disorders, experience with patients, and sensitivity to people. These are perhaps the most valuable qualities to look for in a therapist. A personal experience with an eating disorder is never a substitute for rigorous education and training.

A GOOD MATCH

Sometimes it is a good idea for the eating-disordered person to have consultations with a few different people. This can provide the feel of how different people work. It is important that the "match" between therapist and client be a good one. A client needs to feel she can trust this person. It is, after all, going to be a long and hard journey together; the more comfortable she is at the outset, the more likely she will be able to stick with it during the more difficult moments of treatment and thus the more effective her therapy will be.

WHEN IT'S A POOR MATCH

It is not uncommon for a patient to feel unsure about a therapist in the beginning of treatment. The new patient doesn't know much about the therapist and needs time to build trust. But sometimes the relationship just may not be a "good match." All too often, patients assume that discomfort about therapy is part of *their* problem. The person in treatment should not negate feelings of discomfort or mistrust. Her own intuition can be a useful resource and should be respected.

Usually the best bet is to give the therapy at least three or four sessions before a decision to leave is made. During these sessions, the patient should tell the therapist about her uneasiness. Sometimes voicing these apprehensions allows for a discussion that can abate the discomfort. If this doesn't happen, however, and mistrust and uneasiness continue, a consultation with someone else is in order.

The person in treatment needs to know it's okay to leave. A simple, "I appreciate your efforts, but it doesn't seem to be the right match," should end the relationship amicably. Some therapists may want to meet one or more additional times to see what has gone wrong or to have a chance to end the relationship comfortably. This is common practice. But if the person in therapy is unhappy, ending the liaison should not drag on too long.

WHAT TO EXPECT FROM TREATMENT

How Long Will It Take?

Once someone has found a therapist she likes, this is often the start of a long process toward recovery. The most frequent question we are asked is, "How long will it take?" Unfortunately this is also one of the hardest to answer. The time it takes depends upon many factors.

The duration of the eating disorder will certainly be a determining factor: the shorter its history, the more likely and more quickly recovery is possible. A 14-year-old who has been bulimic for under a year is more likely to benefit from therapy than a 30-year-old who has been bulimic since her college days. This does *not* mean that therapy will be ineffective for the 30-year-old, but it would most likely take longer before you saw an abatement in the symptoms. The severity of the problem is also a big factor. Some people, for example, vomit once or twice a week after having a big meal. Others spend most of their waking hours eating and getting rid of food. For this latter group, the eating disorder is a much more active part of one's daily life, and in these situations it will obviously take a much longer time.

Other addictions, such as drug or alcohol dependency, other psychological problems, or difficulties in the family (such as substance abuse, incest, or domestic problems) will also add to the complications and therefore the length of therapy.

Change takes time. An entrenched eating disorder is a very serious condition and treatment typically involves years, not months. Some people expect that when the eating disturbance goes away, psychotherapy is over. This is not true. The process of psychotherapy helps a person resolve the emotional dilemmas that led them to food in the first place. This process only fully begins when the eating itself is less of an issue. When someone is in treatment, she needs to develop her own pace of recovery.

What Behavior Changes Can You Expect to See?

When someone enters therapy, that does not necessarily mean that the eating disorder will lessen in a predictable manner. Sometimes people initially increase the bingeing or purging in a last-ditch attempt to hold onto the behavior before they have to give it up. Others stop immediately, only to begin self-destructive eating patterns again once they start to feel emotions they've kept hidden for years. Others fluctuate on and off for years before they show signs of lasting change.

You cannot evaluate the benefits of therapy solely on the basis of changes in the eating disorder itself. Sometimes quick improvements in the eating patterns are short-lived, prompted by a display of "white-knuckle" willpower or a wish to please the therapist. Developing a trusting relationship, expressing feelings, and feeling better about oneself have to be established before a more sustained change in the eating can occur. These less observable changes are crucial as a basis of lasting change and long-term growth.

What Mood Changes Can You Expect to See?

"The first year of Katrin's therapy was hell," Grace and Jim Williams told us about their 16-year-old anorexic daughter.

> We expected that once she was in therapy, things would get better. But it didn't go that way. Not only did Katrin continue to starve but she became a complete misery to be around. Suddenly she decided it was okay to tell everyone what she thought of them; going way beyond being honest, she was really nasty. And her moods were intolerable—one day sullen, one day angry. All we would want to do is stay out of her way. Things got a lot better after the first year, but that beginning time was horrible.

Katrin's family's experience differed from that of Alice's, an 18-year-old bulimic. Alice's parents told us that when Alice started to see someone, it was as though a black cloud had been lifted from the whole family: "Her mood brightened. She was visibly relieved, which made us all feel better."

There is no way of predicting how therapy will affect someone. It is a time when new behaviors will be attempted, new emotions come to the surface. Don't rush to make judgments.

How to Be Helpful

How to be most helpful to someone in treatment will vary from person to person. One 24-year-old woman, Jacki, told us that she felt badly that her parents never asked how she was doing in therapy. It made her feel shameful about going, as if this were an embarrassment to everyone. Her parents, on the other hand, wanted to know how she was doing, but were afraid that if they asked Jacki would get angry. (It wouldn't be the first time they had been told to mind their own business.) So Jacki and her parents silently misunderstood one another and uncomfortably walked on eggshells whenever they got together.

If someone you know is entering therapy, ask her how involved she'd like you to be. Can you ask her how she's doing? What should you do if you're worried? Should you contact the therapist? Discuss your feelings openly, and be willing to accept whatever answer the person in therapy gives you. This will certainly ease the discomfort often felt when someone you care about enters therapy, and together, the two of you can anticipate how you'd like to handle potential difficult spots before they arise.

When You're Not Sure About the Progress of Therapy

As with Grace and Jim Williams, it is sometimes hard to believe that therapy is doing any good for the person you know. Perhaps she is upset, still eating disordered, and seems no better than before.

The first thing to do is to ask her how therapy is going. If she tells you she is happy with her therapist and feels she's making progress, it might be best to pull back and not force the issue. You might leave the door open for her to speak with you if she'd like, but it is not the time to insist on a change in therapy. In fact, if you're paying for the therapy, you should anticipate this possibility beforehand and be prepared that even though *you* may not like the results, if the person in therapy is encouraged, it is important not to interfere. Often the changes that occur are subtle at first and will be much more noticeable to the person in therapy than to anyone observing her.

What If No Therapist Is the Right One?

For some proportion of eating-disordered people, therapy is *not* going to help. They may remain in a therapy that is not progressing. Or they may jump from therapist to therapist, program to program, disappointed that no one can help. These individuals have a very deep sense of dissatisfaction with everything and everyone around them. They are overwhelmed by their own pain, and if they go to a therapist, it is with the hope for a process that is swift and painless—a "magical solution" to the problem.

Therapy, however, is not magical. The process of developing a relationship with a therapist can be difficult and anxiety-ridden, especially for people who have little capacity to trust others. The process of knowing themselves better can be frightening and foreign, and they resist it at every turn. No matter what type of treatment, there must be a commitment on the patient's part to the work. When the patient cannot make this commitment, the therapy will not succeed.

Some eating-disordered people are in this situation. They will continue on a chronic course of disturbed eating and change will be marginal. These people will have very disturbed eating patterns for the rest of their lives, without being able to let therapy be of help.

For relatives and friends, these situations are most difficult. The helplessness and frustrations that this type of situation engenders are enormous. No matter how severe the situation, there is nothing anyone can do to make a person stick with or benefit from therapy. Hospitalization can be utilized if the situation becomes an emergency, but you cannot force someone to change.

It is a terrible experience to watch someone you care about suffer and know there is nothing you can do. If you are facing such a crisis, you should not try to do it alone. It is time for you to seek help for yourself.

WHAT ABOUT YOU?—TAKING CARE OF YOURSELF

Regardless of whether the person you care about is making use of therapy, and no matter how minor or severe the situation, you are still going to be left with questions, concerns, and fears of your own.

If the person is not in treatment and you're not sure if a serious problem exists, read Chapters 4 and 5, and consider consulting a professional or group. However, regardless of whether someone is or is not in treatment, having to accept the reality of the problem, the limitations of what you can do, and the limitations of what you can expect from therapy can leave you frightened, angry, and worried. You will need a place to voice your concerns and to learn how to make an independent life for yourself. Often you will need support to stay out of the other person's problems. Perhaps you may be confused as to how to respond to the changing messages you are given by that person as she changes. Or you might be struggling with serious life problems and/or addictions of your own. We have found it invaluable for parents, spouses, even friends at times, to meet with a therapist themselves or to join a support group for significant others.

Therapy

Therapy is an important and sometimes crucial tool in helping you to step back from someone else's problem, accept your limitations in being able to help, consider your own personal difficulties, and move on with your life.

It is very common for the parents and spouses of eating-disordered people to find that they have somehow become dependent on the symptomatic person and her behavior. Brenda Jones, for example, noticed that when Wendy, her 16-year-old anorexic daughter, recovered it was hard for her and her husband to go back to what their life had been before Wendy's illness. Their marriage had revolved around Wendy. Now that she was off going about her life, the Joneses had to work hard to rebuild a life together. Brenda spoke about it this way:

> We hadn't talked about anything but Wendy or done anything but worry about her for so long. In therapy, we were given assignments to spend time together talking about anything but

our daughter. Because we'd been so involved with Wendy, it took an "outsider" to remind us that our own marriage was being neglected. The therapist was able to suggest specific things we could do that would help us be a couple again, not just parents.

Support Groups

Support groups can be enormously helpful for families or couples in which there is an eating disorder. Such groups can be educational and help you feel less alone with the problems you encounter as the other person goes through the process of recovery.

The Resources listed at the back of the book can help you locate support groups in your area. If there are none available, the organizations listed will help you establish one. You may be quite surprised to discover how many other people in your area are struggling with these same problems.

As the eating-disordered person progresses in her recovery, your relationship with her will change. The demands and expectations of the relationship will shift. This is a good place to help you evaluate those changes and allow you to explore and express the feelings you have as the process continues.

Joel, the 28-year-old husband of Sarah, a 26-year-old anorexic, had spent months trying to get his wife to eat and believed Sarah was the only one in the relationship with a problem. Sarah's therapist suggested Joel attend the group. Joel spoke about the first time he went to a support group for families:

> I heard people talking about their relationships, how they planned meals, nagged their wives or daughters about eating, kept setting up rules about how someone had to eat. I thought how controlling they were. By the middle of the group, though, I realized they were talking about the same kinds of things I would do to Sarah and I thought, "Sarah's not the only one with a problem."

Just listening to other husbands in similar situations made me have to think about how I was handling my own relationship. I wasn't the saint I thought I was.

Information and Education

There are newsletters from various organizations that are available to keep you abreast of up-to-date information. Such literature is not only educational; it also provides a forum of ideas and experiences, and can keep you from feeling isolated. There are now national hotlines that you or the eating-disordered person can call for 24-hour help. Use the resource list to find these numbers.

PART III

Using New Strategies

7

WHAT TO DO ABOUT THE PROBLEMS WITH FOOD

Practical Advice for Disengaging From the Eating Disorder

When someone you care about has an eating disorder, regardless of whether or not she is in treatment, you are bound to have questions regarding how to handle food and weight issues. For example, what should you do about her binges? If she's refusing to eat, should you make her eat? Should you say anything if you think she's gaining too much weight? Who should do the shopping? Often parents, spouses, or friends attempt to deal with these matters by trying to change or control the sufferer's eating or purging patterns. This never works. It usually results in relentless control battles. Or sometimes the behavior is changed but only temporarily. When the sufferer's own motivation is not encouraged you will find that when your control lets up, she returns to the problematic behaviors.

This chapter offers practical advice about what you should do regarding the bingeing, starving, purging, and obsessions with weight that you are confronted with on a daily basis. The approach offered encourages you to disentangle yourself from the problems with food and to engage with the person in ways that will encourage her to become responsible for her actions and the consequences of her behavior. She is then free to make lasting changes in her behavior and in her relationships. The strategies discussed will help you to encourage change while minimizing the destructive impact of the eating disorder on your relationship, your life, and your living situation.

The work that needs to be done is part of a broader process, often undertaken with the guidance of a therapist or support group. Disengaging from the eating disorder, examining the reasons why you have stayed involved, and moving on to a healthier relationship are three parts of the process. When your focus is not riveted on the symptoms of the eating disorder, you are in a good position to make the necessary shifts in other areas—changes that will lead to a relationship that is mutually respectful and allows for the feelings and growth of all participants.

While you cannot make someone stop bingeing or starving, there are many things you can do now to make the situation easier for everyone involved. Disengaging from issues with food is the place to begin. This chapter will tell you how to manage your daily living situation (sharing a household), money and finances, eating out, entertaining, and giving advice and opinions.

GETTING PERSPECTIVE

Ron Sklar, a 32-year-old successful businessman, married to Lauren, 25, spoke about the struggle he had after Lauren's release from the hospital for anorexia.

> As part of Lauren's treatment in the hospital, we were in couples therapy. The therapist told me to stay out of anything to do with Lauren's food or weight.
>
> Before she was hospitalized, I was very involved. I would ask her what she ate for lunch and I would spend time preparing dinners I thought she'd like. If she ate one lamb chop, I'd beg her to eat two. She looked so skeletal, so I'd try to find out her weight. All of these maneuvers made her silently furious and none of them made her eat. She just got thinner and thinner.
>
> We'd had plenty of problems between us before Lauren

> became anorexic, but during that year the anorexia took precedence over everything. It was all I thought about.
>
> Now I don't get involved in what she eats. At home in the evenings I've stopped asking her what she's eaten during the day. I can tell she's gaining weight so that helps me to be quiet. Our whole marriage I've felt so responsible for what Lauren feels that keeping quiet is the hardest thing I've ever had to do.

In order to be able to disentangle yourself from food issues you must accept your own limitations. You will not be able to make someone eat or stop her from bingeing. It is a part of the recovery process that you resolve your wishes to do so. The feelings you have of powerlessness, helplessness, and frustration are natural, realistic reactions to a problem you have little control over. Regardless of your good intentions, your attempts to control someone else's behavior always makes the problem worse and interferes with her capacities to change. The person you *can* change is *you*. In this chapter we show you how.

The first step is to remove yourself from the problem. Allow the sufferer to make choices about her behavior unencumbered by power struggles and control battles.

RULE #1 ***Accept your limitations.***

Michael and Melissa Fine are both successful lawyers in their 40s. They are used to success. They were taught that if you really want something, nothing should get in your way. When their 16-year-old daughter Sherrie became bulimic, it was the one thing they couldn't conquer and it drove them crazy. For the first time in their lives they felt like failures. Michael put it this way:

> Melissa and I decided the best way for us both to have exciting careers and still have a family was to have only one child. After Sherrie was born, we were still able to travel and enjoy all the same things we'd done before.

We took on parenting the way we did everything—with all our energy. We spent hours with Sherrie when she was little helping her develop every skill we considered important. When Sherrie started school, she was the brightest and best student. Melissa and I helped her with her homework, her science projects, her book reports. Our home was the hangout for all Sherrie's friends. When she was older and had trouble with a boyfriend, we would talk and help her figure out a solution to the problem.

Sherrie's becoming bulimic was the biggest shock of our lives. But we'd weathered lots of other things; Melissa and I could handle this too. Boy, were we wrong! I'm ashamed to think now how long we tried to take care of the bulimia ourselves. We developed food regimes and bathroom schedules and made it the focus of our lives. The more time we spent on trying to control Sherrie's bingeing and purging, the worse it got.

Finally we went to therapy. It's hard for Melissa and me to give up on the idea that we can't control Sherrie's eating. It's difficult for us to not feel like failures.

RULE #2 ***Accept the other person's right to an independent life. Don't take charge.***

You can offer opinions and suggestions and exert an influence based on your relationship to the person. But each person ultimately has to make her own choices about how to conduct her life.

Until you can accept Rules 1 and 2, you will not be able to disengage from the eating problem sufficiently for change to take place. John and Mary Brown were unable to pull out of their daughter Tracey's bulimia. When Tracey's therapist told them to leave Tracey's eating to her, the Browns were not pleased. "If she would just make up her mind to stop, she could. She's being stubborn," said John to the therapist. Mary worked hard to get Tracey to stop, hoping to calm John's annoyance.

The idea that the bulimia was more powerful than Tracey's willpower was contrary to the family's values. John had made it professionally as a successful attorney after an impoverished childhood. He put himself through law school at night while working days. Mary raised her three daughters and then went back to teaching, the profession she had left to marry and raise her family. The Browns had overcome many obstacles in their lives and they saw Tracey's problem as her not having enough self-control. They were determined to help her in the ways they believed would work.

No matter how many times they were prevailed upon to leave the problem to Tracey, they could not let it go. There always seemed to be another strategy they hadn't tried. John felt if they persisted, they could get Tracey to stop. The Browns could not accept their powerlessness in this situation.

Tracey dropped out of treatment and tried hard to cooperate with her parents' attempts to help her. This went on for years and the Browns remain entangled in Tracey's problem even now.

Tracey lives alone now, but talks to her parents weekly about her eating habits. She lets them know when she's had "good days" and when she's had "bad days." Tracey's eating problem has remained the focus in her relationship with her parents—a focus that prevents both sides from separating and growing.

In another family, the Johnsons, Maggie Johnson's ability to change her behavior allowed her daughter Sarah the room to take charge of her own eating with much better results.

Maggie's response to her daughter Sarah's confession of vomiting was to take Sarah to their physician and then to the therapist he recommended for evaluation. Maggie was not unaccustomed to tough times. Having been left by her husband when Sarah was 1½ years old, she was used to working hard at achieving the comforts she and Sarah enjoyed. Having herself been the daughter of an alcoholic mother, Maggie knew independence and survival from an early age. Her strong commitment and sense of responsibility have been qualities that she's relied on throughout her life. She used these in dealing with Sarah's problems now. Sarah's therapist told Maggie to leave all food decisions up to Sarah herself. That turned out to be much easier said than done, as Maggie quickly found out.

> I'm used to doing things, not *not* doing things, as Sarah's doctor requested. Sarah is 16 and I felt she needed me. It was a long, hard struggle to realize she needed me in a different way than planning her meals and ensuring she wouldn't vomit. For weeks I didn't want to leave her alone at night, when she was most prone to bingeing. I had to learn to trust Sarah, not that she wouldn't binge, but to deal with this particular behavior in her own way. I had to have faith that I had instilled in her enough strength to fight the battle on her own—and win! The only way to let her know I believed she could do it was to let her do it.

In time, Maggie's faith in her own capacities allowed her to believe in Sarah's. "Of course I still worry. How can I stop? But with the help of friends and family, I was able to leave Sarah alone to get a grip on her bulimia."

In order for the eating-disordered person to get well, her problems with food need to be disentangled from all other issues. She needs to be the one making decisions about her food intake and weight. Even if she feels it is out of control, you are *not* the one to take charge. The more control you assume for her, the less she will have to face this problem herself and the longer it will go on.

If you know she is under a physician's and a therapist's care, it will make it easier for you to step back. But regardless of whether she is in treatment or not, you need to step out of the issues about food and weight that inevitably come up.

In the following pages we apply Rules 1 and 2 to the areas of daily living which seem to be the most problematic in dealing with someone who has an eating disorder: household responsibilities, money and finances, social outings, and giving advice.

SHARING A HOUSEHOLD

When sharing a household with an eating-disordered person, the problems that arise about food and related household chores need solutions that respect everyone's rights but do not encourage or provoke the symptomatic behavior.

Household rules will differ depending on your relationship to the eating-disordered person. If the symptomatic person is your daughter, you are in charge of the household, but her age will determine the number and kinds of rules you establish. In a marriage, one spouse does not make rules for another. There is give and take that ideally establishes a comfortable arrangement for both people. For roommates, expenses and household responsibilities are shared jointly by everyone living in the house.

Everyone who lives with an eating-disordered person must face the issue of what kind and how much food to keep in the house. Yet there is enormous confusion about the "right" solution.

Some people we've spoken with keep the house bare of "binge foods"—sweets, pasta, bread, and the like—hoping the bingeing will be curtailed by the absence of such foods. In other households, closets are locked to keep food safe from the binger. Still others keep the house well stocked, hoping the bulimic or compulsive overeater will refrain from "public" binges. And in some households the missing food is simply replaced and everyone accommodates to the situation as though nothing is amiss.

RULE #3 ***Don't purchase (or avoid purchasing) food solely to accommodate the eating-disordered person.***

Household food is to be shared by everyone. However, binge foods are to be supplied by the binger, not by you. Housemates are not to be deprived of foods they enjoy despite the possible temptation to the binger. On the other hand, "health" food, diet food, or the like should not suddenly be introduced as part of the household diet to entice the binger to eat better.

When the Mortons discovered their 16-year-old daughter Patricia was bulimic, Mrs. Morton stopped buying any snack food and went from shopping once a week to shopping three times a week so there would never be a big supply of food in the house at one time.

This made Mr. Morton and their two sons furious at Patricia because there was no snack food at home. Besides, they argued, it didn't stop Patricia from bingeing. What it did do was make Patricia feel even worse because now everyone was angry at her.

If your daughter, spouse, or roommate is anorexic, you may be tempted to have food on hand that may entice her to eat or foods you know she used to enjoy. Unless it is at her request, do *not* provide food with the purpose of seducing her to eat. It won't work. In the Morton family, all attempts to keep healthy food available for the household failed in changing Patricia's bingeing.

It is crucial that the eating-disordered person not be the focus of the household's food decisions. You may feel like you are helping her by eliminating all sweets from the house. This is not help. What you are doing is preventing her from facing the seriousness of her problem and thwarting her motivation to do something about it.

In some households it is helpful to establish food shelves for each household member. Members choose foods they want for themselves and these become nonshared items. If these items are missing or eaten by the eating-disordered person, she is responsible for replacing them. In response to the suggestion that the Mortons have separate food shelves, they devised the following plan:

- Mrs. Morton would shop once a week. Common food would be kept in its regular place.
- Five shelves were marked, one for each family member, and the food on that shelf was only for that person.
- Mrs. Morton asked each week what everyone wanted for his/her shelf. The Mortons had set a $5.00 limit on how much would be spent on each person's individual food.
- Everyone agreed not to eat food from anyone else's shelf unless he/she asked permission.

As part of this plan it was agreed among the family members, including Patricia, that if Patricia ate food from someone else's food shelf, she was required to replace it and forfeit a part of her allowance equivalent to the cost of the food.

RULE #4 ***Each household member decides individually what he or she will or will not eat. No one should be forced to eat anything nor be restricted in what can be eaten.***

Do not encourage the eating-disordered person to eat foods she may not want. On the other hand, do not withhold foods from her because they are fattening or unhealthy. Making someone else's diet decisions in the home leaves her unprepared for making those decisions outside the home.

Questions like "Do you want a taste?" or "Would it satisfy your craving just to have one bite?" are also not helpful and should be avoided.

RULE #5 ***Don't make mealtimes a battleground.***

Mealtimes need not be tense. The eating-disordered person should be treated like everyone else and invited to join you at meals if this is how the household generally functions. If she chooses not to come to the table, make it clear that she needn't eat, but you would like to have her company. Say it in a calm voice and if she still won't come, say, "Okay, but I hope you'll join us next time." Don't stop asking her to join you, even if she keeps refusing.

If she is joining you for the meal, whoever is cooking can tell her what is being prepared and ask if she'll have some. If she says no, she should be free to prepare her own meal (don't do it for her). If desserts have been a part of your family meals, they should not be eliminated. But don't serve any to the eating-disordered person without asking her first. If you know desserts present a problem for her, tell her beforehand you will be serving dessert and she is free to leave if that is disturbing to her. After all, you wouldn't offer a drink to an alcoholic.

Do *not* make suggestions about what the person can or cannot eat. Let her decide.

Jenny, a 32-year-old compulsive overeater, described what mealtimes had been like at home:

Mother would always prepare a diet dinner if I were present. I ate those meals—tuna stuffed in a tomato, no mayonnaise, or plain broiled fish and carrots—feeling like I was in a hospital. It made me so mad. I'd eat what I was served but all the while I was thinking about the cookies I had stashed in my room.

RULE #6 ***Be willing to negotiate household chores involving food.***

Food shopping and cooking are two of the common household chores that involve food. These can be problematic.

In some households the eating-disordered person may be responsible for cooking or food shopping either all the time or on a rotating basis. If this is uncomfortable for the household member with the eating disorder, consider swapping chores for something that does not involve food.

One mother told us of her 16-year-old bulimic daughter Ellie's attempts to shop for the family food. When Ellie was in a phase of trying to control her eating, the foods she'd bring home would be all low fat, no salt, and sugarless. When she was in a phase of being prone to bingeing, she would bring home substantial amounts of bread, pasta, and chocolate.

The family spoke and decided that her household chore should be changed to doing the laundry. Not being confronted with choosing food every week made Ellie feel better. The family was relieved not to be directly affected by her problems with food.

RULE #7 ***The eating-disordered person is responsible for her behavior whenever it affects others.***

BATHROOM MESSES

If someone is vomiting, they are responsible for leaving the bathroom clean and usable for the next person. This is inflexible and not negotiable!

Mrs. Jones agreed with this philosophy. After her daughter Dotty vomited her breakfast, Mrs. Jones would insist she clean the toilets, with an eye for detail. Dotty would "Yes, Mom," and "Okay, Mom," till she was late for school. Mrs. Jones did not want to interfere with Dotty's education and felt that school came first. Since she couldn't bear to leave the bathroom as it was on most mornings, she ended up cleaning it herself.

We were firm when Mrs. Jones told us of the morning ritual. Dotty must clean up *before* she goes to school. She alone must bear the consequences of her behavior, even if that means being late for school, missing a class, or even failing.

You are not to take on the eating-disordered person's responsibilities or ease the consequences of her behavior. Such "help" prevents her from accepting responsibility for herself and growing up.

REPLACING FOODS

If someone binges, she is responsible for leaving the kitchen clean and usable. This includes replacing the foods. If a binge has depleted household or shared supplies of food, these must be replaced in time to be available to others.

If someone feels she has free reign over everyone's food with no consequences, this can be an uncomfortably powerful position. One 17-year-old told her support group she felt as though she was "getting away with murder" in response to her parents' continual replenishment of the food she ate. This was not a position about which she felt pleased.

A plan is necessary for how these situations are to be dealt with.

DEVELOPING A CONTINGENCY PLAN

Rules are useless if you can't enforce them. Along with making rules, you also need to have a plan in effect in case they're broken. What you can do about broken rules depends on your relationship to the person and her age. If you are the parent of a child who lives at home and is financially dependent on you, you have more power and different options than if the person is your spouse or roommate.

The Simons, parents of a 14-year-old bulimic, Abigail, called us because their daughter continually woke in the middle of the night and binged on all the available food. The Simons were distraught: on many mornings they opened the refrigerator to nearly empty shelves. The Simons felt they had no control over Abigail and were at a loss about what to do.

We reminded them that they gave her an allowance, bought all her clothes, and had control over her comings and goings. A plan was developed whereby Abigail would pay her parents for the food she binged on from the money she earned baby-sitting. If she depleted these funds, money was to be deducted from her allowance. If these funds were also used up, she was given tasks around the house apart from her usual household responsibilities. Each task was given a monetary value and she could work off her food debt by doing various chores.

Instituting consequences helps the eating-disordered person take stock of what she is doing and develop responsibility for her behavior.

If the person you are concerned about is a friend or a spouse, negotiate a plan whereby the eating-disordered person is responsible for her behavior.

Sophie and Caron were roommates. Caron's bingeing affected Sophie because Caron ate all the food. They negotiated a plan whereby Caron would contribute an additional $50 a month toward the household budget. At first Caron put off paying Sophie, even though she had agreed to do so. Certainly Sophie could not punish Caron. What she could and did do, however, was to let Caron know she was putting a strain on their friendship. The "consequence," in effect, was the breach that would ultimately occur if Caron would not be responsible in the contract and the relationship. Sophie talked to her and because Caron valued the friendship, she was no longer reluctant to keep the agreement they made.

In another situation between roommates where the issue was a dirty bathroom, the eating-disordered roommate agreed to pay for a cleaning person to come in twice a week. She knew that if she didn't keep to this contract, she would most likely lose her roommate and this was not something she wanted to see happen.

A contingency plan is like a business agreement. You establish with the eating-disordered person, in clear and simple terms, what the agreement is. This includes spelling out what the actual consequences of her behavior will be. These are the principles that will help you in developing a contingency plan:

• ***Use a contingency plan only in situations where the behavior directly affects you.*** Do *not* use it to control eating or purging behavior that does not directly interfere with your day-to-day life.

• ***Be sure the consequences are realistic and enforceable.*** If you are parents of a minor, a financial penalty is a useful one. If your daughter is too young and doesn't have money, then do what the Simons did and assign a value to different household chores till the penalty is paid.

Another consequence that can be used, if it is realistic, is having the person actually replace the food. In Abigail's case this was not possible. They lived in the suburbs and Abigail had no way to get to a store independently.

With a child, the consequence may be in terms of forfeiting some freedom, e.g., she may lose her rights for a Friday night out. This variety of consequence is often more powerful than a monetary one with teenagers.

• ***Be consistent.*** If you "give in" and don't keep the contract the effectiveness of all future contracts will be lost. Be prepared to stick to your guns. Expect to be tested. At the outset of a new plan, the person will want to see if you really mean it.

Familiar excuses that you may make to avoid enforcing a contingency plan may be: "All right, we'll let it go this time but the *next* time our agreement holds" or "I would fine you, but I know you have no money." When you hear yourself saying these or, better still, thinking these phrases, *stop yourself*. Every time you avoid enforcing a consequence you are letting the person know that she can avoid consequences and responsibilities.

• ***Don't apologize for enforcing your plan.*** You were not the one who acted irresponsibly. Expect an angry response to the penalty—ignore it. The Simons were told no matter how much Abigail objected, yelled, or cried, they were to deduct the money from her allowance to replace binge food. We warned them that their daughter might try to wear them down, but eventually if they held their position, she would learn they meant what they said, and they would learn how to use their authority to everyone's benefit.

• ***Don't hold a grudge.*** Once you have carried through with your plan and the person has paid for what she's done (in the manner agreed upon), then the punishment is over and the episode is to be forgotten. Abigail did binge and the Simons deducted the money from her allowance, but continued to be angry at Abigail for bingeing. We told them that the decrease in her allowance was enough and if Abigail got the sense that paying back for the food didn't change her parents' feelings, it would be ineffective as a plan. Don't keep bringing up past infractions.

• ***Change the plan as the person changes.*** A plan must be flexible so there is a response to the individual's change. For example, if you have made separate shelves in your house so that the individual is responsible for what she eats, then you can negotiate a time limit for that setup. If after a certain period there is no problem with the person eating food that is not hers, you can discontinue the separate shelves. In situations where a time limit has not been set for the contract and you notice that changes have been maintained, let her know that you've noticed her efforts. Ask her if she'd like to change the contract that has been set up or if she prefers to keep it going for the time being.

DON'T MAKE EXCUSES FOR HER

Sometimes eating-disordered behavior can have more dire effects than a messy bathroom or missing food. Loss of a job, loss of friends, or school problems may result from the irresponsible behavior that is often connected with a binge and/or purge. Do not provide excuses or help cover up for the eating-disordered person; you are only prolonging the problem.

Laurie wanted to help when her roommate and good friend Carla asked her for a favor. Carla had a particularly bad episode of vomiting that left her with a very swollen face and in a very depressed mood. She did not want to face her colleagues at work feeling and looking the way she did. She asked Laurie to call her boss for her and to tell her boss that she had a terrible cold. Laurie did. Several weeks later Carla asked her to phone in and say she had a bad stomach virus. Feeling unnerved by the whole situation of living with Carla, Laurie attended a support group for family and friends of eating-disordered people. She told of her predicament there. She was advised strongly and unanimously to stop making it easier for Carla. The longer Carla could run from the various consequences of her problem, the worse it was for her.

"It was a hard lesson," Laurie told us. "I thought lying for Carla was an act of friendship. Now I see that a real friend would not help her hide from the truth. When she asks me, I tell her that because I care about her, I cannot help her that way."

RULE #8 *Do not monitor someone else's behavior for them (even if you are invited to).**

It is not uncommon, when someone at home has an eating disorder, for family life to revolve around it. A teenager may ask her folks to stay at home in the evenings so she won't be tempted to binge (an activity she will only do in private). In other cases you may prefer not leaving the other person vulnerable to the temptations of the kitchen.

Decisions about whether you are going out or staying home should be based on how you would like to spend the day or evening.

* The exception to this is in extreme cases when someone is afraid she may harm herself. In these situations you should be acting under the supervision of a professional.

The decision should not be based on being available to control someone's eating.

It may seem cruel to go out when someone is asking you to stay and help her, but that type of "help" only leads to an overdependence that can be crippling. This does not encourage the person to develop her own sense of control. It is more respectful and loving to support the person's own attempts to help herself than for you to be the watchkeeper.

You may be invited to monitor someone else's behavior in other ways. She may want you to keep track of her weight, or report to you what she has eaten. Refuse to do these things. Tell her you understand no one can make big changes by themselves and she should seek the appropriate help in support groups or treatment. (See Chapter 6 on "Seeking Help.")

Questions and Answers on Sharing a Household

The following are common questions regarding household rules:

Q. I found my 15-year-old daughter's laxatives in the bathroom last week. She is in treatment for anorexia, but still uses laxatives to "flatten her stomach" when she eats. I threw them out. Was that the wrong thing to do?

A. Don't go searching through your daughter's private things, such as her purse or drawers. However, if she leaves laxatives or other items, such as diet pills or diuretics, in a noticeable place like a bathroom shelf, then do remove them and comment. It may be a cry for help. Say, "I see you're still taking laxatives. I worry about your health when you do that and wish you would stop." As in all cases of anorexia, your daughter needs medical attention. Be sure the physician and her therapist know about the laxatives. Let your daughter know you are contacting them. (If she were not already in therapy, we would suggest reading Chapter 4, "No More Secrets," for advice as to how to proceed.)

Q. My wife was hospitalized for anorexia. She's been out of the hospital for two months. The other day I noticed she had bought diet foods for the house and she's eating less at meals. The last time I called her therapist without telling my wife, she got furious at me. But I'm scared she's going to lose too much weight if I don't do something. What do you suggest?

A. Tell your wife the changes you've seen in her eating habits. Explain the feelings it generates in you when you notice that behavior. Say it is important that she do something about it, and suggest she speak with her therapist. Explain that it is difficult for you to stay out of her eating if she's not talking to her therapist about it. You need reassurance that she is aware she's having a problem. If you are in therapy together, bring this issue up in your couples' session.

Q. What about having a rule that our daughter can do whatever she wants outside of our house, but in our house no bingeing or purging is allowed?

A. Only make rules you can enforce. Unenforceable rules make you ineffective, and the more of them you establish, the worse the situation will become. Trying to stop your child from bingeing and purging is impossible. Stick with the rules on replacing the food from the binge and cleaning up from the purge. Those rules are enforceable.

Q. My husband and I are divorced and my daughter has been diagnosed as being bulimic. The therapist has told us not to replace food our daughter eats and to make her pay us back if she takes other family members' food. We have joint custody and when our daughter is at my house, I can enforce the rule, but my ex-husband is unable to do it. What can I do?

A. It is difficult when you don't live together to control what happens in your ex-husband's home. You may not be able to do anything. Tell him how important it is for your daughter to be responsible for her bingeing. Talk with your ex-husband about the necessity for him to enforce limits with your daughter. Tell him you know how much he cares about your daughter, but this isn't helping her. Suggest he attend a support group for parents. Finally, make sure you get the support you need too. Divorced families present complicated situations; don't expect to be able to make it all work on your own.

Q. Our daughter is 25 years old and bulimic. She lives with us and binges and purges often. She devours all the food in the house and leaves the bathroom a mess. All our attempts to make her responsible for replacing the food or cleaning up her mess have failed. She refuses to go into therapy. What can we do?

A. Discuss together as a couple the idea of your daughter living elsewhere. As a 25-year-old, she is an adult and can live on her own. If she refuses to accept the rules of your home, you can ask her to leave. This may be hard for you as you may feel you are abandoning her. By not responding to her negative behavior, however, you are teaching her that she can act any way she wants with no consequences. Tell her you are not helping her get well or become independent by putting up with this behavior. You would be willing to help her by letting her continue to live with you if she were using this support to work on her problem in therapy. Since she is not, you cannot let it go on.

Seek support for you and your husband in couples counseling or in a support group.

Q. We have begun using separate shelves for each person's favorite foods. However, our 15-year-old daughter is constantly buying food that she doesn't eat. If she is going to buy special foods, shouldn't she be responsible for not letting these foods go to waste?

A. Someone with an eating disorder is initially going to feel awkward and confused about making decisions concerning what she'd like to eat. She is going to have to experiment with learning her own tastes, the amount of food she needs, and the types of foods she will enjoy or feel comfortable with. She may need to know that more food is available than she actually wants. Expect that food may very well go to waste at times. (You may put an upper limit on what gets spent.)

Q. What should I say when my wife, who is trying not to binge or eat desserts, asks if she can have a taste of my dessert?

A. Why not? Remember, it is not your responsibility to decide what she should or shouldn't be eating. If you are uncomfortable with this, you might tell her that you feel awkward given that you know of her wish to avoid sweets. Ask her what she feels would be most helpful for you to say in those instances. Don't feel that you need to know better than she what the best thing to say would be.

Q. I am married to a woman who is bulimic and in treatment for her disorder. When she shops, she doesn't buy desserts because she fears bingeing on them. However, she knows I enjoy these foods as do our three children. Isn't it her responsibility to care about our needs, particularly those of our children, as well as her own?

A. Not necessarily. There are times when the business of being a wife or mother may not be able to be carried on as usual. This is one of them. Sending someone who is eating-disordered to buy desserts is not unlike sending an alcoholic to a liquor store. This is a time where you should take over and be the one to buy desserts you and the children like. While you need not be deprived of these foods, it should not be up to someone with a "food problem" to have to choose desserts for the household. Food shopping may not be the best task for her. Switch tasks; you do the food shopping and let her manage some other household chores.

Q. I am trying to stay out of my roommate's problem with bulimia. She's in treatment for that. But when she uses the bathroom, she leaves it a mess—she never really cleans up completely after she makes herself vomit. I don't want to interfere in her treatment, but this is hard to live with. What can I do? I can't punish her.

A. A roommate is a peer. Talk to her the way you would to any of your other friends. State your discomfort with the situation and your need to have a clean bathroom. Tell her you admire her decision to get help for her bulimia, but you need to feel comfortable in your own house. You want to be able to support her through this rough time, but when you walk into a dirty bathroom, it makes you angry at her, and then it is difficult for you to be helpful.

Negotiate a contingency plan with her. See pages 153–157 for help and examples as to how to proceed.

Q. My girl friend and I have set up a program that I think might work. She has to tell me every time she binges. She initiated this idea and feels that just the idea of someone else knowing will inhibit her bingeing. It seems to be helping. Should I continue doing it?

A. It has been our experience that this is not an arrangement that works on a long-term basis. Initially, having to confess may make the person binge less. But since bingeing and purging are often an attempt to feel in control of a part of one's life, putting someone else in charge eliminates that feeling of control. Then, paradoxically, the only way the person can regain control is to start bingeing and purging again—and there you are, in a control battle with your girl friend over her eating. There are other ways to show her you care about her. We recommend you back out of hearing her confessions. Say, "I'm sorry, but your eating is up to you. I care about you and wish you would not binge, but I can't stop you. However, if you feel like bingeing and want to call me instead, we could talk about what's upsetting you or do something that we'd both enjoy."

You might suggest she try working with a therapist or a support group so she has a place to discuss her bingeing.

MONEY AND FINANCES

If you are in a position of either sharing expenses with or controlling the expenses of someone with an eating disorder, then no doubt the eating disorder has affected decisions or provoked questions about money.

One husband complained to us about taking his wife out to dinner. He felt as though he might as well throw $30.00 down the toilet instead of paying for food that faced the same fate. The waste of money infuriated him, but he didn't know what to do to change the situation.

A frustrated father wanted to know if he should reduce his 15-year-old son's allowance. The money inevitably went to food, and the father felt as though he was standing by helplessly, watching his son sink deeper and deeper into a pit of overeating.

Parents have asked us whether it would be indulging their daughter's problems by financially contributing to wardrobes of varying sizes. One mother, Mrs. Hanes, told us in a family session that she normally enjoyed shopping with Linda, her 17-year-old daughter. At those times they could take off for an afternoon, have lunch together, and talk (and laugh!) casually as they went from store to store. Mrs. Hanes enjoyed being able to treat Linda to a dress or shirt, and Linda also appreciated the time together. At this point, though, Mrs. Hanes was reluctant to initiate or even partake in these previously enjoyable moments. Linda's weight fluctuated so rapidly these days that Mrs. Hanes thought it frivolous to spend money on clothes that might be too big or too small in a month or two. Besides, she wasn't sure if she would be encouraging Linda's weight obsessions by buying new clothes. Both Linda and Mrs. Hanes missed the time together, but recently no one mentioned it—even the thought of shopping aroused too much tension.

Money presents a particular problem in relationships where an eating disorder is present. It is an area in which you may have control that can directly affect the eating-disordered person's behavior. It is a part of the relationship that can easily be abused. And in so many cases the attempts to help the other person can turn into a misuse of this power.

RULE #9 ***Do not use money to control another person's eating behavior.***

If the person you're concerned about weren't eating-disordered, what would you feel was appropriate behavior regarding payments, allowances, and shared expenses? For a child, give an allowance that is based on her age and related to responsibilities in the house, not determined by the fact that she has an eating disorder. You might talk to parents of classmates to find out what allowances her peers receive.

In the case of the father with an overweight son, the father must decide what he feels is an appropriate amount of money for someone his son's age. If the son decides to spend his allowance on food, that is the son's choice. However, the father needs to be consistent and unyielding toward his son's inevitable requests for more money. This can be tough when the son asks for more money to go to the movies with friends; his father wants him to enjoy himself. But in order for his son to be taught the consequences of his behavior, the father must stand firm.

Mrs. Hanes had to decide whether she'd still like to treat Linda to a clothing gift (no matter what the clothing size) or if shopping for clothes was too "heated." If so, Mrs. Hanes and Linda would pick another activity. It's important to discuss this frankly and openly.

We know of many families in which the daughters have been offered money for pounds lost. Don't do this! This never works and will only increase your daughter's feelings of failure in the long run. Additionally, it treats her serious eating problem as if it were simply a lack of motivation. This resembles a bribe and usurps the person's own inner commitments to making changes.

There *are* times when money can and should be used as leverage to encourage a child's seeking treatment for her disorder. This was discussed in Chapter 5 and is different from trying to control someone's eating behaviors. When money is considered as leverage, professional guidance should direct your behaviors.

If your spouse has an eating disorder, you will need to negotiate finances as a team and together come up with a plan that is mutually agreeable. The husband's questions about paying for dinners with his bulimic wife should be answered in terms of the couple's mutual understandings and compromises regarding how money is spent in the family, not based on his wife's eating disorder.

Roommates and friends can run into trouble around money as

well. Andrea had lent Lynn, her roommate and a compulsive overeater, $500 over the previous year for different weight loss programs. Ordinarily Andrea would not lend out so much money, but she felt her friend was in trouble and needed her help. Lynn's failure to stick to the weight loss programs enraged Andrea, and she told Lynn if she did not lose 20 pounds within the next month she wanted all her money back.

Unfortunately, it is not uncommon to find people embroiled financially in their friends' food and weight problems. Andrea was advised to make future decisions about whether or not to lend Lynn money in the same way she would decide this for other friends. And the plan for payback should be decided in advance.

We helped Lynn and Andrea work out a repayment system for the $500, whereby Lynn made monthly payments over the next 18 months regardless of her success or failure in losing weight.

In general, the overall task is to separate out decisions about money from decisions that are made as attempts to govern, monitor, or control someone else's eating behavior.

Questions and Answers Regarding Money and Finances

Q. My daughter is bulimic. She spends all her allowance on food. I won't give her any more money when she asks me for it. I tell her that's all the money she gets and she has to make choices about what she spends it on. Then she goes to my husband and asks him and he always gives it to her. What should I do?

A. It is important that you and your husband act as a team. You won't be able to make any effective rules if you don't back each other up. Talk with him about the message he's sending her by giving her more money. Tell him that you know your daughter's health is very important to him but that unwittingly he's supporting her in her bingeing. You know he doesn't want to do that and that's why it's important that he not give her any more than her allowance.

Q. Our 17-year-old bulimic daughter is stealing money from my wife, our younger son, and myself. Money is missing and we know it's her, but we don't know what to do. We ask her about it, but she keeps denying it and the money keeps disappearing. What can we do?

A. Stealing is serious business. Contact a family therapist to help you know how to proceed. In the meantime, as difficult as it may sound, you need to put locks on your bedroom doors and keep your money and your valuables in there at all times, especially when your daughter is home and you're not. Tell her it's very upsetting to you that she's stealing and lying, but until it stops, you're going to protect yourselves. Keep careful track of how much money you have. Otherwise, it's easy not to notice when $5 or $10 are missing. Each time you discover money is missing, confront her again. Tell her you want to help her and you don't like locking up your house, but you know she's taking the money.

Q. When our daughter turned 16, we gave her a credit card. Our agreement was that she ask us before she used the card. For months she had been responsible about using it, but recently she has been charging clothes and not asking us first. Also we see the bills but never the clothes, so we think she may be selling them to get money to buy food. We just recently found out from her that she's bulimic. What should we do?

A. Tell your daughter that the original agreement you had about the credit card still stands. The next time there is a charge on it that you did not approve prior to the card being used, you will suspend her use of the credit card. In this way she has an opportunity to control her use of it by herself first.

Q. Our daughter is 26 years old and lives in her own apartment. She earns a good salary, but is always asking us for money. We couldn't figure out where the money was going. She wasn't using it for vacations or clothes, and her rent isn't that high. Then we found she was bulimic and she needed the money to buy food for binges. She's still asking us for money. What should we do?

A. Tell her you know she makes enough money to support herself and you're proud of her ability to do that. However, you are concerned about her bulimia and do not want to support her bingeing by giving her money. Recommend therapy and if she cannot afford it, then tell her, if it's realistic for you, that is something you'd be willing to help her with, but paying for food is not something you can agree to.

Q. Our 16-year-old daughter was picked up for shoplifting food. Should we be responsible for the lawyer's fees?

A. Just giving her the money for the lawyer avoids teaching her the consequences of her behavior. Lend it to her and set up a contract for her to pay you back. This arrangement may necessitate her getting a job so she can earn the money.

Q. My wife is bulimic and is spending most of our money on food. She does not earn any money herself. Before this started, I would just give her my paycheck and she would run the household, which included caring for our two young children. Now I feel she's wasting money. How can I stop her from spending the money so freely?

A. Talk to your wife about your concern. Tell her you cannot afford to have her spending that much money on food and that it is depleting the family's resources. For now, since she seems unable to handle the money, you are going to have to take charge of the finances. Decide together what is a reasonable amount to spend for food for a family of four. If it is decided that she can't shop for food right now, then you will need to do that task.

Your wife should still have money that is for her personal use which you should not interfere with. If she decides to spend that on food, that is her business.

Q. My roommate eats all the food in our apartment. We made separate shelves and our arrangement was that she wouldn't eat any of my food, but she does it anyway. It's really a burden for me financially. What can I do?

A. Tell her you cannot support her bingeing and that it is interfering in your life. You cannot afford to supply her with food. Arrange that she pay you for missing food. If she doesn't and is generally uncooperative, tell her you will not be able to continue living with her.

Q. My roommate has been borrowing money from me and not paying me back. This is new behavior. I know she's bulimic, but I can't afford to lend her money that I don't get back. What should I do?

A. Tell your roommate just that—you can't afford to "lend" her money which is turning out to be a gift. Tell her you won't lend her any more and you want her to pay you back what she already owes you. If she doesn't have the money, work out a plan with her for repayment that is agreeable to both of you.

Q. My wife and I both work so she has her own paycheck. She's bulimic and spends most of it on food. We need her money for our household expenses, so the bingeing is bad for us financially. What can I do?

A. Talk to her about how her bingeing is affecting you financially. Figure out what money you need to run your household and how much each of you needs to contribute from your salaries. When you are each paid, put that amount of money into a joint account. You will need to be in charge of the joint money, but make sure each of you has some separate money so that your wife can contribute to your home but still have control over some of her money. In this way, if she chooses to spend it on food, it will only affect her.

EATING OUT, ENTERTAINING, AND FOOD

Going out for lunch, dinner, a drink, or coffee is a natural and pleasant time-honored way to spend time with someone. But such accepted social activities with someone with an eating disorder can easily become fraught with tensions and anxieties for both parties.

When Kathy first told her friends she was bulimic, they were afraid to suggest going out for dinner together. "Suddenly I had fifty offers to go to the movies. You can't talk to someone in the movies." Kathy's friends were walking on eggshells. This is common. After all, you don't want to make matters worse.

Janis's experience was at the other end of the spectrum. "Every time a friend suggested having a meal together, I would get panic-stricken. I was too afraid I'd put my friend off by saying no and I was terrified of eating in public. I would spend the entire week focused on the dinner, what I would do, what would I eat, would I vomit?"

RULE #10 *Do not anticipate someone else's needs. Ask!*

You cannot know and should not anticipate for someone else what will cause discomfort. For example, clothes shopping can be as anxiety provoking as eating for someone preoccupied with weight. The only way to be sure is to ask. Be willing to negotiate. There are many activities you can share with someone that are not food or weight related. Consider museums, lectures, long walks.

Try not to take things personally. It is not to hurt you that the person is not eating. When you feel hurt, it means the food problem is escalating to a problem in your relationship. (See Chapter 8.) Respect that the person is unable to comfortably be in a restaurant situation; this is similar to a sober alcoholic who does not want to spend time in a bar. When the person feels more in control, she may wish to resume this activity.

RULE #11 *Don't make eating out a battle of wills.*

This is tricky business if you love to eat out and your spouse is uncomfortable eating in restaurants. Talk with her about it. Can she be in a restaurant without eating? Are there certain restaurants that feel "safer" for her than others?

You may find you're uncomfortable if your companion is not eating and you are. Don't push her to eat to ease your discomfort, and next time plan to do something else together.

Perhaps you have to entertain for professional reasons and you need your wife (or husband) to attend. If she is willing to join you at your business dinners, try to appreciate that she is being as co-operative as possible. It is too much to ask her to eat the way you want her to. If her eating habits are disturbing, then don't ask her to accompany you.

If you are a parent and your child refuses to eat, you may decide not to take her with you when you go out to a restaurant. If you feel you will be uncomfortable, it is better to leave her at home.

Questions and Answers Regarding Eating Out and Entertaining

Q. When we entertain now, my wife won't eat in front of anyone. But after everyone leaves she eats all the leftovers. She says she's too nervous to eat publicly. I wish she'd just relax and enjoy herself. What should I do?

A. Talk with your wife about whether entertaining is too stressful for her right now. Find out what is harder for her—entertaining at home or in restaurants. It may be that neither situation is comfortable and you will have to hold back on entertaining with her for now. Talk with her about a plan that will make things easier for her. Tell her it is important to you that you have a social life, but for now maybe you can do things with other people that don't involve eating, such as going to concerts, plays, or movies.

Q. My wife is anorexic, but not at a dangerous weight. She hates going out to restaurants, but I have to for business purposes. She's agreed to accompany me, but I'm worried because she has strange eating habits that are noticeable to other people and I'm worried about what my associates will think. What should I do?

A. This is a time when you have a decision to make. You cannot ask your wife to change her eating habits or worries about food. (If she could, she would without your asking her to.) You must decide either to have her accompany you and eat (or not eat) as she wishes. Or you will have to attend these dinners alone.

Q. My wife is bulimic and in therapy, but she still won't eat anything at family functions. Both my parents and her parents are asking me what's wrong. I've started making all kinds of excuses for why we can't attend, but I don't think I can keep this up much longer. What should I do?

A. Discuss with your wife whether she wants anyone in the family to know about her bulimia, and if so, whom? If she wants to tell someone, let it be up to her, not you, to discuss the bulimia with that person. When questions are asked of you, tell your parents and in-laws that they should ask your wife. Then she can decide what she wants to say and you won't be caught in the middle.

Q. My 15-year-old daughter is anorexic. Whenever we go to my mother's house or to a family function, my mother is always on my back about how little my daughter eats. I've been begging my daughter to please eat for my sake so I won't be put in this embarrassing situation. My daughter still won't eat and it's making things worse between us. What should I do?

A. You need to decide how involved you want your mother to be in your relationship with your daughter. You may want to tell her about your daughter's anorexia. On the other hand, telling your mother may make a situation worse, depending on how helpful your mother is in situations like this. But don't ask your daughter to help negotiate your relationship with your mother. The issue here is really between you and your mother. You have to be in control of it and to set limits on your mother's involvement. You can simply and firmly tell her that you don't want her to ask you any more questions about your daughter's eating behavior.

GIVING ADVICE AND OPINIONS

People close to someone with an eating disorder tell us about the quandary they feel when asked for advice and opinions. "How do I look?" "What should I do?" "Am I too fat?" "Am I too thin?" How do you respond to such questions?

RULE #12 *Do not offer advice or opinions.*

People with eating disorders are often searching for approval from those around them. It is very tempting to reassure them that they look fine or offer your advice about weight or clothes. It may also be tempting to tell them to lose weight if they are overweight or in other ways influence their behavior with suggestions.

These requests are signs of anxiety and insecurity. Your reassurances or suggestions may at best provide temporary relief. But in the long run they further interfere with the persons' developing their own capacities for judgment and self-worth.

Be supportive. Tell the person you care about them and feel badly when they emphasize their weight and looks to the exclusion of their other qualities and traits.

RULE #13 *Do not play therapist.*

Be on the lookout to see if you have taken on the role of therapist or professional, thereby minimizing the need for your daughter, wife, or friend to talk to someone on the outside. Do you feel the burden of having to say the "right" thing, ask the "right" questions, listen to unending concerns about eating with the hope of easing the problem? If you notice yourself doing this, step back from taking on these responsibilities and tell the other person you cannot help her in this way. This will encourage her to look elsewhere for help. Regardless of whether she is in treatment or not, stepping back will also ease the burden you are inevitably feeling and relieve some stress in the relationship. You cannot provide the help you would like to. There is no way for you to be objective or sufficiently detached in this situation. We know that it is quite difficult to step back. You may feel you are abandoning the person you care about. Be assured this is not the case. When she talks about her troubles with food and/or weight, remind her that you know these preoccupations indicate she is feeling badly about herself. There are ways of resolving those feelings and achieving a more positive sense of herself and, as much as you care, you're not the best person to help her out with these matters.

RULE #14 ***Do not comment about someone's weight and looks.***

Telling someone with an eating disorder that they look good or thin is not necessarily received as a compliment. Such statements can be understood to mean that their looks and weight are being observed and assessed. And while at the moment they may meet with approval, these remarks can generate a great deal of anxiety about how they have looked previously and how they will look in the future. While you may give a compliment in an offhand manner or mean it to be supportive, it can have effects far beyond your intent.

Barbara, a 27-year-old compulsive overeater, put it this way:

> I know this sounds overly sensitive on my part, but my boss is always telling me when he thinks I look good. The other day he told me he thought I looked pretty thin—and it got me *angry*! It made me think that he must have thought I looked fat before that and then I was annoyed that he's always noticing. I'm worried enough about my weight as it is—I wish he wouldn't make these comments. It makes me feel that if I'm not at a weight he likes, he's quietly criticizing me in his head. I feel like I'm under a microscope.

Questions and Answers Regarding Advice and Opinions

Q. My daughter often asks me, "Am I too fat?" or "Do you think I should lose weight?" She *is* overweight and I've been telling her to lose weight, but nothing changes and I'm completely frustrated.

A. Do not feel compelled to answer your daughter's questions. While you may care a great deal about her looks and weight, telling her so is not in her best interests. Chances are she already knows how you feel and getting you to say so only increases her anxiety and concern regarding a subject about which she is already overly worried. It is important that she determine for herself what her weight should be.

Do tell her that you care about how she feels and that what is most important to you is how *she* feels about her weight. She has to figure out how she wants to look and what is standing in the way of her own goals. Psychotherapy can help her do this.

Q. My daughter is bulimic. Both my husband and I are very conscious about our appearance. It does bother us when she gains weight. But we don't want her to control her weight by vomiting. What should we do?

A. Don't make comments to her about how much she weighs. You may be putting a lot of pressure on her. Pay attention to how much you talk about weight and appearance in the family. How important is looking good to you? Sometimes your own family values may make it difficult for you to shift away from a focus on looks and weight. If this is your situation you may need to do some work on your own emphasis on appearance. It is harming your child. This work is often best done in therapy.

Q. My husband eats constantly. He was a very heavy child but lost weight before we got engaged. Now he is gaining weight steadily. He asks if I'm still attracted to him. I say yes because I don't think it should be up to me to tell him to lose weight. But I'm not being truthful with him. Should I say anything?

A. Yes. Tell him how you feel about his attractiveness to you. If asked, you might say, "I love you, but I find you more attractive when you're slimmer." This may seem hard to do and perhaps cruel, but hiding your feelings is worse. Be sure you say it in a gentle, loving way. In the case of a sexual partner, attractiveness is a part of the relationship and an answer is called for. Note that you would not be advised to respond this way in a parent-child relationship or a friendship.

Q. I hear my daughter vomiting in the bathroom. What should I say or do? She is in treatment and seems to be progressing. Should I leave it alone?

A. Tell her you heard her vomiting. Then say, "How are you feeling? Is there anything you would like to talk to me about?" It is important she know you are not ignoring the problem. If she prefers not to discuss it, that is all right.

Q. My daughter who is overweight and constantly eating asked me if she should go to Weight Watchers. She also wants me to come with her. She says it will be easier to go together. What should I do?

A. If she wants to go, then you can certainly support that. If she is shy about going alone, you may want to help by joining her for the *first* meeting, but once she is settled, go your separate ways. If you decide going to Weight Watchers is something you'd like to do for yourself, then go ahead—but to a different meeting. Going together can pull you into her struggles with food. Also, by going, you may be putting yourself in a competitive situation with your daughter where there can be a contest about who lost the most weight or who has the best eating habits. Develop other ways to spend time together.

Q. We don't get involved in our daughter's eating. However, every year we send her to a health spa to lose weight. Should we keep doing this?

A. Is it your idea to send your daughter to the spa or does she ask you to do it? If it is your idea, then you are sending her a message that you are unhappy with her weight and you are still involved in the problem. Stop sending her to a spa with the intent of helping her lose weight. You can discuss other vacation options with her, but they should be about having fun, not losing weight.

Even if it is her idea, it is not in anyone's best interests for you to spend your money that way. It will only increase your investment in her weight. Tell her that losing weight is her business, but paying for the spa makes it your business and you don't want to be involved in this way. If she still wants to go to a spa, she should pay for it herself.

Q. My teenage daughter thinks she's too fat to date, and so she refuses any boy who asks her out. I keep trying to tell her she looks fine, but she won't pay any attention to me. What should I do?

A. The extent of her fears and insecurities are beyond the help of a little reassurance. There is nothing you can do to make her date. Tell her you want her to be in therapy or an adolescent support group so she can get some help and not feel so badly about herself.

Q. My roommate who has bulimia keeps breaking dates whenever she feels she is too fat to go out. She's been asking me whether I feel she is inconsiderate when she does this. What should I do?

A. Tell her that in general she's not an inconsiderate person, but in this situation she is behaving that way. To you, this means that she must be having a very hard time with these situations. Her conflict about wanting to date and being afraid of it must be terrible. Suggest she join a support group or speak to a professional about the issues troubling her.

8

WHEN IT'S HARD TO LET GO

Understanding What Keeps You So Involved

Each person who reads this book and applies the guidelines set down in Chapter 7 will have a different experience of disengaging from the eating problem. Your experience will vary on a continuum from that of a relatively easy time making the changes we've suggested to finding it almost impossible, regardless of your best efforts and intentions. In all cases change is a process that occurs over time.

If you find that no matter how hard you try to change, you keep returning to old problems, this is not a sign of weakness or failure on your part. What it likely means is that your involvement has come to serve a purpose for you in your life. Perhaps worrying about the eating-disordered person keeps you from facing even more difficult problems. Perhaps you are relating to the person with the eating disorder the way you have been taught to relate to a parent or sibling in your original family. How deeply involved you are with the eating behaviors will determine how much work you need to do to disengage yourself.

Ginny Stone had been working on being less involved in her daughter Nicky's bouts with bulimia. Nicky, 15 years old, was in treatment and working at resolving her eating difficulties. Mrs. Stone, who attended a support group with her husband, wanted to do what was best for Nicky. But she was having a very hard time of it.

> I've stopped asking Nicky what she's eating and if she's vomiting, but I still go into the bathroom after she's left it to see if she's vomited. I find myself lying in bed at night waiting to hear if Nicky is in the kitchen. Lately I've even begun to look through the waste can in her room for candy wrappers or other signs of a binge.
>
> I want to stop, but I can't. I must be somewhat to blame for her eating disorder. She *is* my kid. I keep wondering if I focused too much on her being thin or if I kept too much food in the house. When Nicky was young, my husband Michael and I fought a lot—maybe that did it—making her feel insecure. In any case, I can't get it out of my head that I brought this on somehow. How can I just sit back and not do anything to make her better?

Mrs. Stone felt she was to blame for Nicky's behavior. Her guilt and belief that to be less involved with the eating problem was an abandonment of her daughter kept her involved in a way that had consequences for them both. It prevented Nicky from being able to take responsibility for her own behavior. It kept Mrs. Stone wrapped up in Nicky's problems to an extent that she could not comfortably put her energy into her own life and marriage.

SIGNS OF OVERINVOLVEMENT

Sometimes your continued involvement will be noticeable to you, as in Mrs. Stone's case. For others, the indications are more subtle. The following are signs to be aware of that indicate difficulty disengaging:

- You have difficulty following through with the rules we discussed in Chapter 7.
- Even though you don't want it to, the eating behavior and/or weight fluctuations of your daughter, spouse, or friend determine how *you* feel during the day, making it a "good day" or a "bad day" for *you*.
- You are preoccupied with the eating-disordered person's behavior.
- Your preoccupation results in neglect of other things you should be doing.
- Acting like a detective, you engage in secretive behavior, looking and listening for signs of bingeing, purging, exercising, or the like.

THE JUSTIFICATIONS

You may feel that your situation is different from others and that there are good reasons for you to keep on top of the eating disorder. There are always fears, ideas, or rationales that justify an involvement. In Mrs. Stone's case, telling herself she was to blame and *should* make it better was the thought that gave momentum to her preoccupation with Nicky. Another woman, Paula, who was married to a compulsive overeater, told us that she could not stop suggesting what her husband should eat because she did not believe he was capable of monitoring his own diet. She was convinced that if she didn't say anything, he'd eat so poorly and get so obese that he would jeopardize his health. "If he dies, it would be my business, wouldn't it?" she asked. "I mean, his dying would certainly affect *my* life!" This rationale kept her embroiled in her husband's eating behavior.

Others stay involved because they feel convinced that the eating-disordered person is doing this to hurt them. "If she cared about me, she would stop," is a phrase we frequently hear.

For example, John told us that his wife Vicky knew how much

it meant to him that she stop bingeing. If she loved him, she wouldn't keep overeating like that. He could not stop arguing with her about the food because he wanted her to see what she was doing to him.

While every one of these people had their reasons for staying involved, the reasons only masked the more meaningful dilemmas and conflicts in their lives. Mrs. Stone was having trouble sorting out her responsibilities as a mother. Was she wedded to some old ideas from her original family? Paula had work to do on why she felt her husband was so incompetent. Was he really? Or was this how she was taught to relate to men? John was measuring Vicky's love for him by what she did or didn't eat. What kept him measuring Vicky's love this way? Was this a holdover from his original family?

Justifications for your involvement may sound good to you on the surface, but they only prolong the eating disorder and keep obscured from you the areas in the relationship and in your own life that need work.

The justifications have the strength that they do because they are fueled by some need you have and probably don't know about to remain invested in the eating disorder. Just as the eating disorder may serve a function for the person with the problem, so too it may be serving a function for you. However, the cost of this to your relationship is high. It keeps you relating to your daughter, spouse, or friend narrowly through her problems with eating and food.

Don't Try to Figure It Out Yourself

The emotional issues that underlie an intractable involvement on your part in the food problem can be multiple and complex. People committed to the treatment of alcoholics have long recognized the need to help the alcoholic's family and friends deal with these issues. Al-Anon was established just for this purpose. The recognition for such support is growing among the eating disorders professional community as well. Often seeking the help of a professional or a support group is the only way to explore and resolve the complicated factors that underlie your involvement.

YOUR INVOLVEMENT: WHAT IT MEANS

There are myriad reasons why people have difficulties disengaging from the problems of others. Each situation is unique. However, in talking with many people about their relationships with eating-disordered people, we have found that there are common factors that seem to influence the disengagement process. The following sections of this chapter discuss these factors and examine some of the situations we have seen.

The Effect of Family Rules

As we discussed in Chapter 3, old family rules often make change difficult. In the same way family rules make it difficult for the eating-disordered person to grow up, they may interfere with your being able to disengage and move on with your life.

In Mrs. Stone's case, these rules were guiding or, more accurately, misguiding her behavior in relation to her daughter. In her family, leaving someone on her own meant you were abandoning them and not fulfilling your job as a parent.

Ronni and Lilly's situation provides another example of how old family rules operate in current relationships. Ronni and Lilly were college roommates. Ronni spent a year with Lilly, over the course of which Lilly's weight dropped from 115 to 85 pounds. Ronni responded to Lilly in much the same way she had to her father when she was living at home.

In Ronni's family, she had been responsible for her father's feelings. When he came home in a bad mood, it was Ronni, not her mother, who would try to cheer him up. She was the one who would ask about his day and sympathize with him about any problems.

Ronni fell into the same role with Lilly. She would often stay with Lilly instead of going to classes. She thought if she could get Lilly to eat then all would be okay. She'd buy "goodies" she knew Lilly liked and leave them around the room. In response to Lilly's questions about how she looked, Ronni would try to build her confidence by telling her she looked fine. She didn't say anything about Lilly's increasing exercise regimes.

Ronni's attempts to help were well-meaning, but enabled Lilly to lose more weight undetected. The more fragile Lilly became, the less Ronni asked of her, and still Lilly did not change. Ronni grew resentful and Lilly became more annoyed as Ronni watched her even more closely.

One afternoon Ronni attended a lecture on eating disorders sponsored by the health services department of the university. Then it struck her that this was different than the circumstances at home. While she may have been able to cheer her father up, she realized that all her attempts to help Lilly failed in the face of Lilly's serious illness. She stopped thinking she could change Lilly on her own, and suggested they go to the health services department and talk to someone there.

It is necessary that you distinguish between action that is truly helpful and behavior that comes from old family rules which may prevent someone from taking responsibility for herself.

The Need for a Smokescreen

An entrenchment in the eating disorder sometimes functions as a smokescreen that obscures other difficulties that may exist in your life.

Mary James, a 39-year-old mother of a bulimic, shared with her support group the way this happened for her:

> My husband Marc and I had a consultation with my daughter Dori's therapist last week. The therapist was concerned because she felt that I was too involved with Dori's eating habits. She asked me what I'd be worrying about if I weren't thinking about Dori. After a long silence and some uncomfortable glances from Marc, I told her that I hated how much my husband drank. I said it so low she didn't even hear me and I had to say it again.

> I feel like I can only deal with one thing at a time—and the truth is I *don't* want to deal with Marc's drinking. I can't bear to think I'm living with an alcoholic.

As long as Mary was involved in her daughter's problem, she could tell herself that it wasn't the time to confront Marc too. However, both her support group and therapist disagreed. Mary was encouraged to attend an Al-Anon meeting and her husband was urged to go to Alcoholics Anonymous. Their therapist told the couple that the issue of drinking could no longer go undiscussed and referred them to a couple's counselor.

Substance abuse is more prevalent in the families of people with eating disorders than in the general population, and frequently a focus on the eating problem hides the drug, alcohol, or other food abuse that may exist among other family members. This cannot be taken lightly. The person with the eating disorder should not have to take care of her problem before other problems are addressed. If you are someone who has worried (even secretly) about your own use (or your spouse's) of food, alcohol, or drugs, it is possible that a focus on someone else's eating disorder might be keeping you from the business *you* need to attend to. Whenever any questions exist regarding drug or alcohol abuse, Alcoholics Anonymous or Narcotics Anonymous meetings (or the "sister" organizations such as Al-Anon) should be attended for information or a source of support, or a professional should be contacted.

Substance abuse, however, is not the only problem that can be obscured by the focus on an eating disorder.

Betty Jo, 20 years old, spoke at a college support group about how her roommate Debbie's eating disorder functioned as a smokescreen for her:

> When everything started happening with Debbie's anorexia, I kind of forgot about my own life. I'd worry about her and be checking all the time for how she was feeling.
>
> It sounds funny now, but it was the calmest I've been in

my life. It was good to worry about someone else and not pay attention to myself. Before, I felt so bad and unable to do anything about it. My parents got divorced when I started college, and they'd each call me to tell me how awful the other one was. I didn't know how to stop them. But Debbie's difficulties gave me an unforeseen excuse to change the subject. I noticed that when I'd talk to them about Debbie, they would get worried about her too and the conversation would focus on her anorexia, not on my parents' mutual complaints about each other.

But once Debbie got into therapy, things changed. She didn't want me to worry about her so much. She made me promise I wouldn't discuss her with my parents. When my parents called, I was back to conversations I had been dreading. One night I spoke to my dorm counselor about it. She suggested I nicely tell my parents that I was happy to talk to them, but I wouldn't listen to criticisms from one about the other. Then if one of them kept it up, I was to say, "I'm sorry, I won't listen to this. I'm hanging up."

After a few horrible calls, I was able to hang up when one of my parents started getting nasty about the other. After a few hang-ups, they both stopped criticizing the other. I was able to see how angry I was at them for doing this and I was thankful I got out of it. I even looked forward to talking with them. As long as I had had Debbie to worry about, I could shut out my own feelings and put my problems on a back burner.

The Need to Fill a Void

The focus on the eating disorder may make up for something missing in your life. In fact, you may not even be aware that something is lacking.

The void may always have existed, or it may be the result of having been focused on someone else to the exclusion of yourself or your other relationships.

Tom was 40 years old when his 13-year-old daughter Molly became anorexic. He and his wife Kathy, 38, spent five years immersed in Molly's problems. They had seen many doctors, followed Molly in and out of hospitals, struggled their way through five painful years of disrupted meals, emotional battles, and the constant fear that their daughter would die. Now it finally looked like the pain was behind them. Molly was settled in treatment and was maintaining a healthy weight. She was able to leave home for the first time and attend college in another state. Kathy and Tom had just received a spirited letter from their daughter. School was fine and it looked like she had even started to date. But Tom remained troubled.

> I woke up one morning and realized that I was scared to death. Kathy and I had been so involved in Molly's problem that we'd done little else for five years but worry about her. I began to think about how different Kathy and I were—she, so quiet and reserved, me, outgoing, driven, always involved in something. I thought of how rarely we spent time together these days. We were always in separate rooms of the house.
>
> Except for the half hour around dinnertime, when we exchanged information about Molly and her older brother who was also away at school, we really didn't have much to talk about. I couldn't even remember the last time we made love. I found myself missing the kids terribly. The house was so quiet now. I got scared that I'd be spending the rest of my life in a dead marriage, just waiting for grandchildren so we'd have something to do.

What dawned on Tom that morning was how, in dealing with Molly's problems, both he and Kathy had been ignoring their marriage. Something was missing and neither he nor Kathy had wanted to face this. As long as the kids were home—and certainly as long as Molly was sick—Tom had no opportunity to feel the deficits in his marriage. But now that Molly was better and just he and Kathy were home, he recognized his long-standing focus on Molly had allowed him to put off the problems he knew were pending in his own life.

Tom and Kathy asked Molly's therapist to recommend a family counselor and the two of them began treatment. With the help of the therapist, they began to work on rebuilding their marriage together.

The situation of Mrs. Kinney and her 18-year-old bulimic daughter is another example of how a void may be filled by attention to the eating-disordered person. Mrs. Kinney was urged by her support group to leave her daughter Ruth's eating and weight problems to Ruth. She had a very hard time of it. The groups suggested she spend more time with her friends and follow through on some of her own independent interests. What soon became apparent was that Mrs. Kinney did not have any friends, and apart from watching TV and her daughter, she had no interests. Her involvement with Ruth was Mrs. Kinney's one contact in an otherwise isolated, withdrawn life. At the urging of the group and for the ultimate benefit of both Ruth and Mrs. Kinney, she went into individual therapy to work on her own fears of people and relationships.

MOVING ON

In order to move on to establishing a healthier relationship with the eating-disordered person, you must take the steps necessary to disengage from the problem. If you are having trouble staying out of the food issues, now is the time to take stock of what your investment is and what keeps you so entrenched.

Don't expect yourself to be able to be objective about this. The reasons for your involvement are often invisible. It is the involvement itself that is the signal that something powerful is at work motivating you. To help you disengage, seek the services of a therapist or a support group.

Only when you can stop your focus on the eating disorder can you find healthier ways to reconnect with the person you care about and address the issues in your relationship that otherwise will remain mishandled or overlooked.

9

DEVELOPING A HEALTHIER RELATIONSHIP

Relating to the Person, Not the Eating Disorder

As you begin to disengage from the eating disorder, you will be able to gain a clearer perspective on your relationship with the sufferer. It's time to put the past behind you, resolve the frustrations and inequities in the relationship, and reestablish and nurture its strengths.

When parents, spouses, and friends disengage themselves from issues with food, we often find that there are several aspects of the relationship that need work. These have to do with communication, responsibilities, rights, and enjoying each other. While there may not be anything you can do to change someone's eating behavior, there are many things you can do to develop new growth, respect, and enjoyment in the relationship with the person you care about.

IMPROVING COMMUNICATION

An important part of any relationship is that of being able to talk with one another honestly and comfortably. This takes effort. An equally difficult part of communication is listening without judging and allowing yourself to hear the feelings and dissatisfactions of the other.

Learning to communicate takes practice, especially if your family rules have emphasized that keeping negative feelings to yourself is a virtue or that pretending everything is fine will make things fine.

Katherine and Phil Martin were having difficulties with their daughter Kelly, who was 16 years old and bulimic.

Katherine told us:

> In our family, we lived by the old adage, "If you don't have something nice to say, don't say anything." When Kelly turned 14, she started disagreeing with us about all sorts of things. She raised her voice all the time. This infuriated both of us, but we didn't know how to respond so we ignored it. Her rage escalated to where she called us names, slammed doors, and broke plates when she was really angry. We tried not to pay attention because of the eating disorder. We didn't want to make things worse.
>
> Phil and I finally went to see a therapist because we just couldn't handle the situation. The therapist encouraged us to regain our right to be respected as parents, but she also pointed out that Kelly had the right to express feelings. Slamming doors and vile language were not considered "expressing feelings." Kelly needed to talk about the differences she had with us without acting like a possessed demon. We in turn had to learn how to listen to her complaints.
>
> The therapist suggested we have family meetings once a week where we could talk together. If someone didn't like a house rule or how someone was being treated, this was the time to bring it up. We told Kelly she could tell us about her anger, but she could not call us names or break dishes. And tell us she did! She had a slew of complaints, some reasonable, some not so reasonable. The tough part for Phil and me was listening to it all and taking Kelly's complaints seriously. We've had to sift through them and actually Kelly has become more reasonable over time. I guess she was like a pressure cooker, holding all that back and then exploding.

Matthew, 34 years old, discussed his difficulties communicating with Monica, his 32-year-old wife and a compulsive overeater:

> Whenever she's upset she cries and then goes and eats—she never gets mad and really tells me what's disturbing her. It's like a guessing game. I find myself walking on eggshells with her.

There were many reasons why this couple had trouble talking with one another but they did not have to do with Monica's eating habits. While Matthew invited Monica to tell him what was bothering her, in fact he would get angry in response to her criticisms. And Monica held back for fear of being too much of a burden to him. She worried he'd leave her if she complained too much.

To start them off, their therapist suggested that they set aside one hour a week, after the children were asleep, to talk. Monica was to have the floor for twenty minutes, and then it was Matthew's turn. Monica was to tell her husband all her gripes without interruption. Matthew's job was to listen but he could not interrupt. Then for the following twenty minutes, Matthew was to talk about how he felt about what was said. If he was upset, this was the time to say it, not while Monica had the floor. The last twenty minutes was to be spent negotiating a plan that would take into consideration both their positions. The following week Matthew was to speak and Monica was to react.

"It was an eye-opener," said Matthew. "I had no idea Monica was so unhappy about so many things and that I could be so defensive. I thought I was a good listener but I really wasn't. I thought the only problem was that Monica couldn't be open with me. But I found out that there was another side to this problem—I had a hard time listening. She still has her problems with bingeing, but it doesn't upset me as much. What matters to me is that we're talking a whole lot more."

Learning to communicate entails both learning to express yourself and learning to listen effectively. Don't let your emotions get in the way of your ability to listen. And remember, focusing on the eating disorder will interfere with *both* communicating and listening.

Guidelines

Here are some general guidelines to keep in mind for improving communication:

- Do not assume someone else's intentions, thoughts, or feelings.
- Do not blame or attack the other person.
- Do not induce guilt. For example, "You're killing me when you do . . ."
- Speak with "I" statements. (See Chapter 4 for a more detailed explanation.)
- Balance your communication—be sure people know what you like as well as what you're unhappy with. Be generous with praise, but only if it's sincere.
- If need be, establish household meetings to pave the way for open communication. Establish ground rules that allow people to speak freely without fear of an angry response or retaliation.
- Be willing to seriously consider others' gripes and to work toward a mutually satisfying agreement.

ESTABLISHING RESPONSIBILITIES

In any marriage, intimate relationship, or household, responsibilities are divided. Sometimes what develops works well and feels fair, other times it doesn't.

As we discussed in Chapter 3, in families in which there is an eating-disordered child, there are often imbalances in the area of establishing responsibilities in the household. Many times parents err in one direction or the other, taking over too many tasks for the children or burdening them with responsibilities beyond their capacities. To make matters more complicated, both situations can exist at the same time. It is not unusual, for example, to find a bulimic teenager whose parents leave her quite on her own scholastically (even if she is doing poorly in school) and at the same time maintain early and strict curfews.

In evaluating the responsibilities your eating-disordered child has, you must realistically consider her age and her capabilities. Do not work around her eating disorder, viewing it as a handicap; this will only discourage her from feeling competent about managing her own life. Helping someone grow up includes allowing her increasing rights and responsibilities regarding decisions about her own life (i.e., what to wear, what friends to have, what activities she can participate in).

Roger Cohn and his wife Patty grappled with this situation with Cynthia, their 16-year-old daughter, before they were seen in family treatment. Cynthia fluctuated between bulimic and anorexiclike behaviors. Roger spoke of their situation this way:

> It was hard for us to think of her as being 16. She always seemed and acted younger. She'd ask our help for almost everything and we were pleased to help her. But it seemed we were doing the same things for her at 16 that we did when she was 4. We thought telling her to try it herself would sound like we weren't being good parents. Cynthia didn't even clean her own room —we did. Every morning my wife would make Cynthia's bed and pick up all the clothing off the floor.
>
> When we began therapy, we had to reevaluate things. The therapist told us that Patty and I had to help Cynthia grow up.
>
> The first rule we established was that Cynthia's room was her responsibility. She could keep it as neat or as messy as she wanted. If she wanted clothes washed she'd have to make sure they were in the laundry bag. We didn't want to see the mess in her room so we asked her to close her bedroom door when she wasn't home. Cynthia would provoke us sometimes by not closing her door. My wife and I are very neat so it wasn't easy to leave her room alone. We insisted that the rest of the house be kept clean. This was common property and Cynthia had to pitch in.
>
> For the first time, we gave Cynthia an allowance. Before

this, whenever she asked for money for anything, we either gave it to her or not, depending on whether we agreed on how she wanted to spend the money. Now she was given $20.00 a week to spend as she pleased. In exchange for her allowance, she was expected to dust and vacuum the living room once a week as well as help with the dishes each night.

Then we worked out a system to handle Cynthia when she left things around the house. She would be asked twice to pick up after herself. If we had to ask a third time, we subtracted $1.00 from her allowance for every item left around the house. We didn't scream. We didn't yell. We just deducted money from her allowance.

We've been doing this for three months, and now that the rules are clearer, Cynthia has become more responsible. We spend much less time arguing and much more time talking with her about other things in her life, like school and boyfriends. I think Patty and I were sort of surprised, too, that someone who had as many problems as Cynthia did—starving, bingeing, fasting—could actually *be* responsible. It's been nice to be able to see our daughter in this new light.

By giving Cynthia more responsibilities, the Cohns were telling her that they felt she was capable of taking care of herself, an important message to support her sense of competency. They were also respecting her as a person with needs, values, and preferences that were different from their own.

In marriages or friendships in which one person is eating disordered, responsibilities may not be fairly divided. When that happens, the balance of responsibilities must be renegotiated between the people involved.

Mark, the 30-year-old husband of Justine, 28, talked about the division of responsibilities in their marriage:

In our relationship, I tended to be the one in control. I like to be the one in charge and Justine went along with that because she felt taken care of. It never occurred to me that she was unhappy. Until Justine became anorexic, things were going fine.

But when Justine stopped eating, I went nuts. It was the first time in our marriage I wasn't in control. Nothing I did made her eat. In the support group she began attending, she was encouraged to make more decisions in our relationship. Now she tells me we have to renegotiate our marriage so it's equal between us and I'm not making all the decisions. I'm not sure whether Justine can make decisions for herself, let alone for the two of us. How is she going to tell me what to do if she can't even figure out what she should eat?

Mark and Justine had a marriage that was based on Mark's need to have someone to take care of and Justine's desire to be taken care of. Ironically, Justine's anorexia was her attempt at doing things *her* way, and yet it also proved to Mark that she was incompetent and needed his help. However, when Mark attended a family support group with Justine, the men in the group urged him not to just see Justine as sick. It was important that Justine learn to take charge even if she was anorexic.

Now Justine and Mark have to renegotiate a marriage based on equality. If they succeed, they will have a chance at a relationship that is enjoyable and pleasurable to them both. In order for change to occur in any relationship, you must be willing to evaluate and balance how decisions are made and how responsibilities are shared. If both parties are not willing to make this change, the marriage will most likely end or remain chronically troubled.

Guidelines

Here are some guidelines for improving the balance of responsibilities in your relationship:

- If you are parents, look at the rules your family has regarding responsibilities. When children or teenagers are involved, you must make sure the responsibilities are appropriate to their age. If you're not sure, consult with friends, teachers, or support groups to find out what responsibilities are typical in your community among children of the same age.

- If there is disagreement between parents and children, parents ultimately set the rules—but not without hearing your child's opinions. When in doubt, speak with other parents or professionals to establish reasonable expectations of your child.
- Between adults, be sure the division of responsibilities is fair and appropriate for everyone involved. Each person's responsibilities should be clearly spelled out so nothing is assumed or taken for granted.
- If there are areas of disagreement, either a household meeting or a planned time to talk can provide a forum for discussion. Usc the guidelines suggested for communication when you hold these meetings.
- Among adults, disagreements with regard to responsibilities should be negotiated openly until a fair arrangement is agreed upon. When difficulties seem insurmountable, a support group or professional advice can provide helpful guidance.

RESPECTING RIGHTS

Imbalances that exist regarding responsibilities inherently create imbalances regarding people's rights. This may include the right to age-appropriate freedoms, to privacy, and, when a child is involved, the right to be taken care of.

As we discussed in Chapter 3, a focus on an eating problem can obscure these rights.

The Right to Grow Up

One problem we commonly see is that when children with eating disorders mature, they are prevented from experiencing the freedoms they should be granted as they get older. In our previous example, we discussed how Cynthia Cohn was not expected to assume responsibilities typical of a 16-year-old. This was not the only way in which she wasn't treated her age. Her father was nervous about her going out on dates or even hanging around with her girl friends in the evenings. As a result, Cynthia had to be in by 10:00 P.M. on weekends. By her parents' standards, this was a fine compromise, but Cynthia ended up feeling like a baby among her friends, all of whom had much later curfews.

Part of the work in the Cohn family was not only considering responsibilities, but reevaluating the rights and freedoms of family members. Having an 10:00 P.M. weekend curfew was unreasonable for a trustworthy 16-year-old in the community where the Cohns lived. The Cohns were urged to speak with other parents of 16-year-olds to find out what curfews they had for their teenagers. After doing this, a 12:00 A.M. curfew was finally decided upon for the weekends, with the compromise that Cynthia would keep her parents informed as to where she was spending her time.

If Cynthia did not respect the curfew, if she did not call or was more than fifteen minutes late, she was grounded one night the next weekend. This was not negotiable. Cynthia could complain, but the agreement would stick. No matter how important the week's missed event might be, if Cynthia was late she had to pay the consequences.

The Cohns were urged not to evaluate Cynthia's rights based on her eating behavior. She was 16 years old, regardless of how or what she ate, and she needed to experience the freedoms that other adolescents her age enjoyed. Her trustworthiness would be based on how she handled these freedoms, *not* on how well she recovered from an eating disorder.

The Right to Be Taken Care Of

Rights not only have to do with letting a child grow up and become independent, but also with protecting her from having to grow up prematurely. A child or teenager has a right to be able to depend on her parents to be there as sources of authority, security, and comfort—without having to ask.

In Rayann's situation, she and her mother were very close. Her mother Susan was very caring and worked hard to provide a good upbringing for her only daughter. Rayann's parents had divorced when she was 3 and neither she nor her mother had seen her father since. Rayann was now 14. Susan felt that she had done the best job she could as a single mother. Rayann had been healthy as a child, did well in school, and was very involved socially with a group of friends whom Susan liked and respected. Only Rayann's bulimia was a clue that something was wrong. When Rayann went into treatment for her eating disorder, Susan joined a mothers' group because she wanted to know what to do to help. Susan describes the outcome of the meetings this way:

> Rayann and I always have been close. She can talk to me when something's on her mind and I am able to talk to her whenever I'm upset. I always thought this was a good thing, but in the group I learned that maybe I had become more of a friend than a parent.
>
> The group helped me notice how much I depended on Rayann to be there for me. I never thought this was bad, but the group felt that it was encouraging Rayann to be responsible for me. There were certain things they said I shouldn't be talking to her about, like how I felt about men and sex, how lonely I was, how much her father had let me down. Not that I should be phony, they told me, but just that these were adult issues and could feel burdensome to a teenager. What was apparent was that Rayann had become my only friend and that as long as I relied on her like a friend, she would feel burdened.

Susan was urged to stay in the group as a way to develop a support network beyond her daughter. The group helped Susan refrain from certain discussions she normally had with Rayann—in particular, sex, men, and her loneliness. As Susan was able to depend on her peers instead of Rayann, she noticed a burden was lifting from her shoulders. While she had enjoyed her closeness with her daughter, she also had often felt shaky—after all, relying on a 14-year-old is not a secure position to be in. With a newfound source of support (the group) and newly felt experiences of security, Susan noticed that she was enjoying her daughter in a different way. She didn't expect as much from Rayann anymore. And she noticed that Rayann, on the other hand, seemed to feel relieved—in fact, it seemed she was turning to her mother more these days with her own questions about guys, school, and clothing. For the first time, Susan felt confident about being a mother, not a peer, to a 14-year-old.

Because Susan sought help in response to Rayann's bulimia instead of just trying to change the eating disorder, she was able to work on the areas in her relationship with her daughter in which she could effect change and be of help.

Because children like Rayann are so quick to fill in and do the jobs asked of them, it is easy to miss how deprived these children feel inside. While they may be very needed and important to their parents, they can also be suffering from neglect, a neglect no one sees. Often it is easy to miss how in need these teenagers are of parents' time and comfort. When this is the case, their rights as children or adolescents are being overlooked.

In another example, Henry Phillips spoke about the relationship he and his wife Connie had with Suzette, their 13-year-old bulimic daughter:

> Connie and I are both professionals. I'm a screenwriter and Connie is an internist. We work long hours and love our careers.
>
> Connie leaves the house early in the morning to make hospital rounds and has office hours until 7:00 P.M. When we eat together, it's around 9:00 P.M. or 10:00 P.M. and Suzette has long since finished. When I am home, I'm often writing.
>
> We've always relied on a live-in housekeeper to keep things running smoothly. Our older son Jeremy, 17, never had any problems. He does well in school, has lots of friends, and the girls are crazy about him.
>
> Everything seemed fine until Suzette became bulimic. This

stopped us in our tracks. We made sure she saw a therapist right away.

Suzette's therapist wanted to see all of us, but we couldn't find a time that all four of us could make. I'll never forget this scene: Connie was on the phone with the therapist and we were looking at our schedules. Suzette was sitting on the couch near the phone and could hear the conversation. The therapist would mention different times and either Connie or I would say, "No, that's not a good time for me." After a few minutes of this, I noticed Suzette was crying.

The therapist must have sensed what was going on and she said, "Your daughter is in serious trouble and you need to make this a priority or things will get worse. Here are the times I can see you. See which will work best for you and call me back tonight."

When Connie got off the phone, Suzette screamed, "You have time for everyone but me." We realized we had better reorganize our lives or Suzette would suffer.

In the Phillips family, Connie and Henry valued their own independence and encouraged this quality in their children. They tried to be responsible parents and when they arranged for treatment for Suzette, they felt they were handling the situation as best they could. But therapy could not do it all. Other aspects of their relationship with Suzette needed attention—they needed to be more available as parents.

In family sessions with the Phillipses, this issue was the main focus of their work. Connie and Henry had to arrange their schedules so they were available to spend more time together as a family. Family dinners were encouraged. Suzette needed and responded well to having the security and closeness of being with her parents.

The Right to Privacy

In the Phillips family, the parents' needs for their independence and private lives interfered with their daughter's need to be taken care of. However, it is important that you not create an imbalance in the opposite direction. In any household or relationship, everyone has a right to some privacy.

In some families or households, time alone may be seen as an insult to other household members or a signal that something is wrong, as opposed to a natural developmental or personal need. If in your family love is measured by involvement and time spent together, you may have trouble establishing privacy for yourself or allowing it for others.

"I remember the first time we decided to shut our bedroom doors at night," said Marlene, a school administrator in her 40s.

> We had been leaving them open since our girls were babies, and somehow it never changed. Now our daughters are 14 and 16. Our oldest, Lydia, protested all along about this open-door policy, but we found it hard to make the change. Somehow it seemed safer to us to leave the doors open. Our support group, however, had a different view and felt strongly that Lydia needed her privacy. After years of being anorexic, she was actively struggling to feel more grown-up and the group felt we needed to support that. At first, I felt that it was unsafe to have Lydia close her door. She was so skinny—what if something happened to her during the night? If she got up and fell, I wouldn't hear it. Her doctor had told me this was ridiculous but I still worried. The group insisted that I treat her according to her age, not according to my fears.
>
> We decided to try it. That first night I lay in bed listening to the silence of the house. Oddly my children felt so far away from me. My husband's steady breathing only made me feel more alone. I thought how crazy this was, that just a shut door could make me feel this way. I think it's the first time I realized that maybe I *was* having a hard time letting them be on their own.

The mere act of closing doors in and of itself is an important stand in allowing for privacy in relationships.

Marlene was willing to make changes in her behavior, to shut doors and to be honest with herself about her own difficulties. Marlene's soul-searching led her to a willingness to respect Lydia's need for independence.

The eating-disordered person is not the only one who needs privacy. Every individual has that right, including parents.

Peggy, a 42-year-old stockbroker, talked about trying to work during her 18-year-old daughter Jane's struggle with bulimia:

> It seemed as though every time I turned around, Jane was calling me. Sometimes she'd call ten times a day. I felt so guilty if I didn't talk to her, but my stomach would tighten and I could feel my anger as soon as I heard her voice on the other end of the line. The phone calls were upsetting. Even after the call was over, I'd have a hard time concentrating on my work. Finally, my boss told me I couldn't do both things. It was impossible to do my job and speak to her that often. I decided to speak with an Employee Assistance Program counselor on the job. We devised the following way to handle Jane's calls:
>
> I set aside time every day when I would talk to Jane outside of work. She lives with me, so we could easily arrange time when I wasn't working. I told Jane that if she wanted to talk to me, we could have breakfast together every morning at 7:30. I didn't care whether she ate, but I wanted her to sit with me.
>
> During that time she could talk about anything that was bothering her. Then she could call me once during my lunch hour between 12:00 and 12:15 P.M. and once after the market closed. In the evenings I'm home. If Jane were home and wanted to speak to me, we could talk then.
>
> If Jane called me at any other time, I was to say I'd speak to her at our next arranged time and then hang up. I was to do that no matter how many times she called. This way, I was available to her, but not controlled by her.
>
> I tried these things out. The first two days were miserable. Jane didn't wake up for breakfast and she never called me during the arranged times. Instead she would call at other times.

> However, after two days of my insisting she call at the arranged times, she slowly started following the schedule. It's now been three weeks and she occasionally calls when she's not supposed to, but I keep to the schedule and I don't feel angry or guilty. There are days now that she doesn't even call at all.
>
> Now that this schedule is working out and I don't resent Jane as much, we seem to be enjoying our time together more. She asks me to do more things with her, like go shopping or to a movie. I spend my time at work without feeling guilty, and we're much less frustrated with one another.

It is not only individuals who need privacy in a relationship. Parents, as a couple, need to be able to establish private time for themselves apart from their children. Without this, both the parents and the child can suffer.

This had been so for many years with the Kasins. Lynn and Eric Kasin, both 43, had been seen for couples' therapy as part of the treatment plan for their 15-year-old bulimic daughter Alicia. At the time the Kasins entered therapy, Alicia was binge-vomiting four or five times daily or she would eat nothing for days at a time.

One of the striking aspects of Lynn and Eric's relationship was how little time they actually spent with one another apart from the children. Eric, a contractor, tended to work late, and when he was home he and Lynn spent most of their time with Alicia.

Lynn and Eric's therapist noted how guilty they felt about spending time away from their daughter. How could they have a good time when she was suffering? The therapist reminded Lynn and Eric that it was not helping the situation for them to focus on their daughter and her problem to the exclusion of their own lives. Lynn and Eric's "rule" about how to be good, caring, close parents was actually preventing Alicia from growing up and keeping them from enjoying their marriage. The therapist suggested that Lynn and Eric go away for the weekend.

At first, the Kasins were enthusiastic about this idea and appreciated the "permission" to go off on their own. They arranged for Eric's mother to take care of Alicia and their two younger children, and they spent a couple of weeks eagerly planning a romantic weekend away.

When the weekend arrived, two hours before they were scheduled to leave, Alicia started to cry and said she didn't want them to go. She threatened not to eat the whole weekend if she had to stay with her grandmother. She had become accustomed to being the center of her parents' activities.

Fortunately, Eric's and Lynn's therapist had predicted this might happen. Alicia was not used to being away from her parents, and consequently feared being without them and on her own. In the past, her parents would not have gone, causing Alicia to believe she could *not* be on her own. This time was different.

Eric and Lynn turned to the plan they had formulated in therapy about what they would do if this happened.

First, they both told Alicia they were still going away.

Second, they said they were sorry she was so upset and that she wasn't going to eat. If on Monday, when they came back, she still wasn't eating and they thought she was in physical danger, they would contact her therapist who would evaluate whether the situation was critical enough for her to need hospitalization.

They then told Eric's mother to make meals the way she normally would and to set a place for Alicia. If Alicia refused to eat, her grandmother shouldn't push it or get into any fights with her. Eric and Lynn would handle the situation when they came home.

Lastly, Eric and Lynn explained that they would call once a day to hear how things were going.

Eric spoke about the weekend:

> It was rough getting out of the house. Alicia was crying, and my poor mother was almost as upset as Alicia. Our two younger kids tried to pretend nothing was happening. We were determined, though. We hadn't been away alone since Alicia was born and we were set on getting the time now.
>
> We had picked this beautiful country inn and it was early spring so the weather was lovely. We worried about Alicia during most of the ride but vowed not to talk about it. As soon as

we got to the inn, we felt better. We decided to eat dinner before we called home. It was delicious and we had a great bottle of wine. When we called home, Alicia had not eaten and refused to come to the phone to talk to us. Saturday we slept late, had a big breakfast, took a long walk, and went shopping. Then we came back to the inn and made love without worrying about interruptions. It was terrific.

That day when we called home, Alicia had eaten dinner but still wouldn't talk to us on the telephone. What was new for us was that even though she hadn't eaten, our Saturday hadn't been spoiled. We were getting along, we had a plan for what to do if Alicia didn't eat, and neither one of us let it ruin our weekend.

For Eric and Lynn, their marriage had been subsumed by their worry about Alicia and they had forgotten the pleasure they could get from each other.

GUIDELINES

Here are some guidelines to help you ensure that everyone's rights are being respected in your relationship:

- If you are parents establishing ground rules for your children, freedoms should be commensurate with age. Check with other parents in your area to see what curfew times are considered reasonable, how much allowance is considered fair, and what other rights and freedoms are granted.
- A child should not be treated as a friend, nor as someone beyond her chronological years. Do not tell your child your marital or sexual problems. If you are doing so, you must STOP. If you have questions in this regard, a peer support group is an excellent way to get help establishing appropriate areas of discussion with your children.
- Children have differing needs in terms of their parents' time. If your child or teenager is complaining that she does not have

enough time with you, listen carefully. She may be right. This may be a sign that you are unwittingly neglecting her. Plan to spend more time with her.

- Individuals in a household have a right to private time and to closed doors.
- Establish clearly what times or areas are off limits to others' calls or visits—and also establish times when you *will* be available. For example, while work is off limits, you might want to make it clear that you will be home for dinners or available to talk during your lunch hour.
- Couples need time alone without children, friends, or relatives. If you find that you and your spouse do not spend enough time alone, set up a plan to have dinner or to go out by yourselves. If you have difficulty doing so, the guidance of a peer group or a professional can help you arrange a plan suitable for you.

STRENGTHENING YOUR RELATIONSHIPS WITH THE EATING-DISORDERED PERSON: HAVING FUN

And finally, don't forget to laugh.

The most effective way of strengthening a relationship with someone is to be able to have fun together. When there is a crisis in a family or relationship, certainly when someone has an eating disorder, this is often the first thing to go. But trouble involving the eating disorder is only one aspect of your relationship. There are still many ways to share interests, feelings, thoughts, and pleasures. Don't forget the many other ways you can enjoy each other and continue to have fun.

"Things were different before my husband and I got married," said Georgette, 33, about Kevin, 38 and a compulsive overeater:

> Everyone loved being with Kevin—especially me. But once we got married, it seemed like I forgot some of that. He would get me so angry because he was always eating or thinking about

food. I was really worried about how much junk he'd eat, and we started to argue about that all the time.

Things got bad between us. We finally saw a couples' therapist. The therapist encouraged me to recall some of the things I had loved about Kevin. He has a great sense of humor and likes to do fun things like going to zoos, amusement parks, the racetrack, all kinds of stuff. So the therapist suggested that we do those things again, and asked Kevin to pick something that was a little crazy, a little offbeat, like the things he used to suggest.

I, in turn, made a vow to shut my mouth about the eating and just enjoy what we planned to do.

It wasn't so easy getting off the food police squad. I started to notice how much I worry all the time. But last month what really hit me was how I'd stopped letting myself enjoy Kevin. We were at an amusement park with my nephews and I could see Kevin was really enjoying himself with the kids. He was so easy and filled with laughter. And me—I was worried about whether he was going to eat hot dogs and cotton candy.

It was as if for the first time I finally understood how involved *I* was with Kevin's eating. Here, everyone else, including Kevin, was having a good time, being silly, having fun. And all *I* could do was worry. Every time I start to worry about Kevin, I think of that day in the amusement park and I'm able to stop.

Last weekend Kevin told me that he noticed I haven't been on his back lately and he thanked me. I can't believe how close I've been feeling to him these days—I wasn't sure that feeling would ever come back.

When Chrissie Small became anorexic at 13, it seemed that the whole family fell apart. Three years later, Maggie, her mother, described how things began to turn around:

For three years, things have been so tumultuous. Our lives revolved around Chrissie, especially when she had to go into the hospital. All our conversations centered on trying to get our daughter to eat. These last few years have felt like a blur—I don't seem to remember anything else except problems.

It's funny, about six months ago, Chrissie got out of the hospital and began to eat normally—but our lives didn't change much. We still mostly talked about Chrissie's anorexia and her progress.

A month later, though, Chrissie got a part in the musical *Grease*, in her high school drama class. She asked us for help in learning her lines and we spent part of our evenings doing that. Even our 14-year-old son Jed got involved. I was sitting there one night and it hit me that we were laughing as a family. I'd forgotten that sound. I'd forgotten that Chrissie had talents. During the time she was anorexic, that was all she was to me —a starving daughter whom I was trying to save.

We had so much fun helping Chrissie with that musical that when our church planned to put on a play for a fund raiser, all of us tried out and got parts. We were having fun again and it felt good.

There is only one basic guideline to regaining fun in your relationship and that is:

- It is okay to enjoy each other no matter whether an eating disorder exists or not.

Enjoying one another may involve pursuing a project or activity that you both enjoy. It may entail setting aside time to be alone with one another—or to join other friends or members of the family in activities that were fun prior to the development of the eating disorder. While you can make an atmosphere more conducive to having fun, while you can plan the time or activity, enjoyment is something that you can't *make* happen. It is a natural process that occurs between people when no obstacles are put in its way. A focus on the eating disorder can become such an obstacle. Notice if this is the case in your relationship and work on removing it.

ON THE ROAD TO RECOVERY: BOTH HERS AND YOURS

Someone with an eating disorder has a long road to recovery. How she manages food and weight issues along the way will be part of her independent struggle to get well. What you do can make a big difference, both for you and for her. If you remain invested in the eating disorder, your involvement can contribute to prolonging the problem. It can also hamper the growth of your relationship.

There are ways, however, in which you can create an environment that allows for a richer, fuller way of relating, and which can minimize the need for the maintenance of a symptom. We have provided you with tools to help you in your efforts. Professionals and support groups can be there as your guides. Don't go it alone. Be patient. And learn to discover the ways in which you and the person you care about can enjoy one another and expand your relationship.

This is not an easy task. But if you continue in your efforts, there is much hope for the future.

We wish you good luck.

SUGGESTED READINGS

Bruch, Hilde. *Eating Disorders: Obesity, Anorexia and the Person Within.* New York: Basic Books, 1973.

———. *The Golden Cage: The Enigma of Anorexia Nervosa.* Cambridge: Harvard University Press, 1978.

Cauwels, Janice M. *Bulimia: The Binge Purge Compulsion.* Garden City, N.Y.: Doubleday, 1983.

Chernin, Kim. *The Obsession: Reflections on the Tyranny of Slenderness.* New York: Harper & Row, 1981.

———. *The Hungry Self: Women, Eating, and Identity.* New York: Harper & Row, 1985.

Crisp, Arthur H. *Anorexia Nervosa: Let Me Be.* London, Toronto, and Sydney: Academic Press; New York and San Francisco: Grune and Stratton, 1980.

Garfinkel, Paul E. and Garner, David M. *Anorexia Nervosa: A Multidimensional Perspective.* New York: Brunner/Mazel, 1982.

Garner, David M. and Garfinkel, Paul E. *Handbook of Psychotherapy for Anorexia Nervosa and Bulimia.* New York: Guilford Press, 1985.

———. *The Role of Drug Treatment for Eating Disorders.* New York: Brunner/Mazel, 1987.

International Journal of Eating Disorders. Michael Strober, ed. New York: Van Nostrand. A quarterly publication.

Hirschmann, Jane R. and Zaphiropoulos, Lela. *Are You Hungry?* New York: New American Library, 1987.

Johnson, Craig and Conners, Mary. *The Etiology and Treatment of Bulimia Nervosa: A Biopsychological Perspective*. New York: Basic Books, 1987.

Kinoy, Barbara; Miller, Estelle B.; Atchley, John A.; and the Book Committee of the American Anorexia/Bulimia Association. *When Will We Laugh Again?: Living and Dealing with Anorexia Nervosa and Bulimia*. New York: Columbia University Press, 1984.

Levenkron, Steven. *Treating and Overcoming Anorexia Nervosa*. New York: Scribner's, 1982; Warner, 1983.

Meehan, Vivian; Wilkes, Norma Jean; and Howard, Heather Lee. *Applying New Attitudes and Directions*. Highland Park, Ill., 1984.

Minuchin, Salvador; Rosman, Bernice L.; and Baker, Lester. *Psychosomatic Families: Anorexia Nervosa in Context*. Cambridge: Harvard University Press, 1978.

Munter, Carol and Hirschmann, Jane R. *Overcoming Overeating*. Reading, Mass.: Addison-Wesley, 1988.

Neuman, Patricia A. and Halvorson, Patricia A. *Anorexia Nervosa and Bulimia: A Handbook for Counselors and Therapists*. New York: Van Nostrand Reinhold, 1983.

Orbach, Susie. *Fat Is a Feminist Issue*. New York: Paddington Press; Berkeley Medallion Books, 1978.

———. *Hunger Strike*. New York and London: W. W. Norton & Company, 1986.

Palazzoli, Mara Selvini. *Self Starvation: From Individual to Family Therapy in the Treatment of Anorexia Nervosa*. Arnold Pomerans, tr. New York and London: Jason Aronson, 1978; London: Human Context Books, Chaucer, 1974.

Root, Maria P.; Fallon, Patricia; and Friedrich, William N. *Bulimia: A Systems Approach to Treatment*. New York and London: W. W. Norton & Company, 1986.

Sours, John A. *Starving to Death in a Sea of Objects: The Anorexia Nervosa Syndrome*. New York and London: Jason Aronson, 1980.

Related Subjects

ALCOHOLISM

Alcoholics Anonymous *(The Big Book)*. AA World Services, Inc., New York, 1955.

Bepko, Claudia and Kreston, Jo A. *The Responsibility Trap: A Blueprint for Treating the Alcoholic Family*. New York: Free Press, 1984.

Dulfano, Celia. *Families, Alcoholism, and Recovery—Ten Stories*. Center City, Minn.: Hazeldon Foundation, 1982.

Maxwell, Ruth. *The Booze Battle*. New York: Praeger Publishers, 1976.

Vaillant, George E. *The Natural History of Alcoholism—Causes, Patterns, and Paths to Recovery*. Cambridge: Harvard University Press, 1983.

CHILDREN OF ALCOHOLICS

Black, Claudia. *It Will Never Happen to Me!* Denver, Colorado: MAC Printing and Publications Division, 1982.

Deutsch, Charles. *Broken Bottles, Broken Dreams*. New York: Teachers College Press, Columbia University, 1982.

Marlin, Emily. *Hope: New Choices and Recovery Strategies for Adult Children of Alcoholics*. New York: Harper & Row, 1987.

Seixas, Judith S. and Youcha, Geraldine. *Children of Alcoholism: A Survivor's Manual*. New York: Crown Publishers, Inc., 1985.

Woititz, Janet G. *Adult Children of Alcoholics*. Hollywood, Fl.: Health Communications, Inc., 1983.

INCEST

Bass, Ellen and Davis, Laura. *The Courage to Heal: A Guide for Women Survivors of Child Sexual Abuse*. New York: Harper & Row, 1988.

CHANGE

Lerner, Harriet Goldhor. *The Dance of Anger: A Woman's Guide to Changing the Patterns of Intimate Relationships*. New York: Harper & Row, 1986.

RESOURCES

National Referral and Self-Help Organizations

The following organizations provide the names of therapists, doctors, outpatient facilities, and hospitals. If they cannot help you locate trained professionals in your area, try contacting state or county mental health associations listed in your local phone directories, or the nearest university hospital.

American Anorexia/Bulimia Association Inc.
133 Cedar Lane
Teaneck, New Jersey
(201) 836-1800

A.A.B.A. was established in 1977 by Estelle Miller to help the families and victims of anorexia and bulimia. They can make referrals nationally and in some foreign countries. There are general public meetings in the Teaneck area that feature a distinguished speaker and are then followed by a support group. They have affiliated support groups in New York, Philadelphia, Virginia, and Florida. If you want to form a self-help support group, they have information packets which tell you how to do so. In addition, they publish a national newsletter, distribute information about anorexia and bulimia, provide speakers to the public, and hold conferences.

ANAD—National Association of Anorexia Nervosa and Associated Disorders
P.O. Box 7
Highland Park, Illinois 60035
(312) 831-3438

ANAD was the first association in America developed for the education and support of individuals and families combating anorexia nervosa and bulimia. It was founded by Vivian Hanson Meehan and Chris Athas. They can make referrals throughout the United States and in some foreign countries. Self-help support groups assisted in their development by ANAD are affiliated with the parent organization and may be found in forty-five states, Canada, West Germany, Austria, and Saudi Arabia. They have a national hotline that provides counseling for victims and family members and referrals to therapists and self-help support groups. The hotline is at the above telephone number and operates Monday through Friday from 9 A.M. to 5 P.M. central time. In addition, they supply a national newsletter, information packets, consumer advocacy, and early detection and education programs.

Anorexia Nervosa and Related Eating Disorders, Inc.
P.O. Box 5112
Eugene, Oregon 97405
(503) 344-1144

Anorexia Nervosa and Related Eating Disorders, Inc. was founded in 1979 by Dr. Jean Rubel. If you call the above number, you will get the answering service. If you leave a message you will be sent an introductory packet. If you want to speak with someone personally, call (503) 686-7372. They provide referrals nationally and in some foreign countries. They have self-help support groups in the Eugene area, and can provide information packets to help you start a support group in your area. In addition, they have a national newsletter, educational booklets, and brochures. They also offer speakers for conferences and seminars. They are affiliated with Sacred Heart Hospital in Eugene, Oregon and offer in-patient, outpatient, and after-care programs.

The National Anorexia Aid Society
5796 Karl Road
Columbus, Ohio 43229
(614) 436-1112

This organization was founded in 1977 by Pat Tilton. They provide referrals in the United States and in some foreign countries. There are self-help support groups in the Columbus area and they will send you a packet for starting a self-help support group in your area. In addition, they publish a national newsletter and educational brochures and provide speakers for conferences and seminars. They have an outpatient facility at the above address that makes an assessment of an individual's needs and has the services of psychiatrists, psychologists, social workers, and dieticians to help with the eating disorder.

The following organization also provides a national newsletter.

Eating Disorders Digest
5625 Government Street
Baton Rouge, Louisiana 70806
(506) 924-4313

Twelve-Step Self-Help Organizations

Overeaters Anonymous Headquarters
World Services Office
4025 Spencer Street, Suite 203
Torrance, California 90503
(213) 542-8363

Alcoholics Anonymous
468 Park Avenue South
New York, New York 10017
(212) 473-6200 (9:00 A.M.–10:00 P.M.)

Al-Anon and Children of Alcoholics are organizations for people whose lives have been affected by someone else's alcohol use. Consult the phone book under Al-Anon or Children of Alcoholics for local organizations. Each state has its own organization.

INDEX